The Poetry of Villon

The Poetry of Villon

JOHN FOX, B.A., D. de l'U.

Lecturer in French
University of Exeter

Thomas Nelson and Sons Ltd

London Edinburgh Paris Melbourne Johannesburg
Toronto and New York

THOMAS NELSON AND SONS LTD
Parkside Works Edinburgh 9
36 Park Street London W1
117 Latrobe Street Melbourne C1

THOMAS NELSON AND SONS (AFRICA) (Pty) LTD
P.O. Box 9881 Johannesburg

THOMAS NELSON AND SONS (CANADA) LTD
91-93 Wellington Street West   Toronto 1

THOMAS NELSON AND SONS
18 East 41st Street New York 17, N.Y.

SOCIÉTÉ FRANÇAISE D'ÉDITIONS NELSON
97 rue Monge Paris 5

————

Foreword

IT has become the tradition to begin a work on Villon in a highly imaginative way. In the opening scene of one, the night angelus bell is tolling dolefully as a thin sly-looking fellow sets out to join his confederates, with whom he has planned to rob the Collège de Navarre. Another begins with the gates of the prison at Meung-sur-Loire clanging shut, leaving a dark-skinned little man blinking in the bright light of day he has not seen for many a month. A third—the most startling of all —makes reference to the pubs off Tottenham Court Road, in which, so we are told, Villon would have felt perfectly at home. Such arresting openings are doubtless called for by the nature of the man and his life, that of his poetry and indeed of the period as a whole. However, I have no intention of playing the game according to these rules. Readers looking for highly spiced reconstructions of this type will find ample material elsewhere. The Vagabond King does not go rollicking through these pages; there are no tavern signs creaking as the wind catches them; no thieves on the prowl in the medieval Latin Quarter; no gay stories of students' rags and conflicts with the arm of the law; no cryptic messages buried deep in the verse; no shadow of the Montfaucon gibbet falling ominously across every page. This monograph is concerned with Villon's poetry, not as an autobiography, but simply as poetry. To be sure, the very nature of the work demands that some account of the life be given: it is quite impossible in the case of Villon to dissociate altogether life and work, as Paul

Valéry has observed in his essay coupling Villon's name with that of Verlaine, but the biographical material will here be reduced to a minimum. What really matters, after all, is the poetry, and the life must throw light on the poetry, not merely *vice versa*.

It would be an exaggeration to claim that the many works on Villon ignore the literary aspects of his poetry. None the less, the fascination exerted by his life and temperament is such that a good number of critical works have tended to lead off at a tangent, away from the actual poetry. Even the more scholarly type of work often evades literary appreciation. The approach in the scholarly sphere has frequently been an historical one, linking Villon's themes with those of earlier centuries, or else dealing, like the more popular works, with the life and times, but with greater attention to accuracy of detail. On the other hand, a philological approach has been followed in numerous articles published in learned periodicals, whose interest is concentrated on the understanding of the linguistic material of the text. The primary concern of historian and philologist alike is not with purely literary criticism, which they view with mistrust since it tends to involve subjective interpretations more than objective analysis. Indeed, the literary appreciation that has appeared on Villon has been of an almost wholly personal kind: 'My idea of Villon' or 'What Villon means to me' has so often been the basic attitude. However, the emergence in the first half of this century of stylistics as a discipline both literary and linguistic has gone some way towards changing the picture, and presents the critic with new methods of studying literature which have something of the objectiveness of the linguistic sciences, and which have reduced to more sensible proportions the purely personal element in criticism. This approach, like any other, is not without shortcomings. Stylistics concerns itself with the effect produced by the various aspects of a work —images, rhythm, sound-patterns, word-order or other features of syntax—but a fragmentary treatment of this nature can never be wholly satisfactory since any work, particularly of poetry, is more than just a sum of its parts. The atmosphere created by a poem as a whole may far outweigh any precise, analysable meaning or intention residing in particular details, and the more the appeal is to the emotions, or the closer the effect is to music, the more is this true. The success of stylistics in achieving an objective analysis must depend to some extent on the particular work that is being studied, but at the very least it will always have the valuable effect of making the text itself the most important object, not just the ideas evoked in the critic's mind by the text, or any other matters which, however interesting or well presented they may be, are fundamentally irrelevant. This alone is a considerable achievement.

The main aim of the present work is to provide a stylistic study of Villon's poetry. This has been prefaced by a brief survey of the variations in attitude towards Villon through the ages, concentrating on the very considerable developments in and near our own day, characterised by a growing awareness of the aesthetic qualities of his verse.

Although intended mainly for the specialist and for university students following an Honours French course, and although it does not set out to be picturesque or popular, this work, it is hoped, will prove of interest to a wider reading public, since Villon has for long been well known on this side of the Channel. So many bilingual editions of his works are available (see Bibliography) that it has not been thought necessary to translate the numerous quotations from his poetry, all of which are based on the most reliable edition at present available, that by Auguste Longnon, revised by Lucien

Foulet and published in the *Classiques français du Moyen Âge* series (4th edition, Paris, 1932).[1]

[1] The various revisions proposed by A. Burger in *Lexique de la langue de Villon* (Geneva-Paris, 1957), and by F. Lecoy in 'Notes sur le texte ou l'interprétation de quelques vers du *Testament* de Villon', *Romania*, 1959, pp. 493-514, have been taken into account. In the quotations from Villon's works *L*=*Le Lais*, *T*=*Testament*, and *PD* = *Poésies Diverses*.

Contents

Acknowledgments

I SHOULD like to take this opportunity of expressing my grateful thanks to Professor J. P. Collas, Professor A. H. Diverres and Professor B. Woledge for the time and trouble they have taken in advising me on various aspects of Villon's poetry. I must add that they would not necessarily wish to associate themselves with all the views expressed in these pages. I am equally indebted to my colleague Dr Philip Yarrow for his constant encouragement, and to Professor R. Niklaus for the interest he has shown in my work.

I should also like to thank Dr W. G. Moore, General Editor of the *Modern Language Review*, for allowing me to quote largely from an article of mine which appeared in that journal in July 1960; and Professor Alfred Ewert, General Editor, for permission to repeat the argument I put forward in an article in *French Studies*, in 1953.

JOHN FOX

Exeter, 16th May, 1961

Introduction

A PARADOX which never fails to fascinate is that François Villon, the most renowned 'bad lad' of an age by no means lacking in rogues and rascals, should be the author of what is, by common consent, the finest lyric poetry to have been written in medieval France. Villon's name is the first one worthy of mention in all French literature, according to Boileau, and however sweeping that statement may be, the wide knowledge of medieval literature possessed today has not altered the fact that Villon is the most popular and widely read poet of pre-Renaissance France. Editions of his poetry, some highly seasoned with grotesque cartoons, some diluted into expurgated translations, some garnished with a rich array of footnotes, appear in the windows of the Paris bookshops side by side with the works of Rabelais, Montaigne, Molière and the other great names of French literature. It is a measure of his genius that his appeal is as much alive today as it was 500 years ago, perhaps even more so. It is not merely the fascination of catching an echo of our own fears and preoccupations in this far-off voice, not merely that it is so easy to sympathise with Villon because like him we all pass through moods of despair and moods of rejoicing, and because like him we are often appalled at the callousness of life and are always ready to conclude that we might just as well make hay while the sun shines. It is not merely that our own pronouncements on ourselves and on life are, like his, so apt to be distorted by self-interest and self-pity, or that, like him, however much we may believe in an after-life, we do not feel at all eager to leave the present world, and have difficulty in accepting the thought that we must one day die. It is more than all that, for the whole complex web of emotions which any individual living in society must weave about himself is here exposed to view. When not concerned with himself Villon is concerned with those around him, the inhabitants of Paris whom he knew as relations, public figures, friends or enemies. His attitude towards each one of them is revealed, whether it be affection, jealousy or hatred, but we learn more about the poet than we do about them, for all his remarks reflect back on his own character and outlook. It is a world of feelings and a world of people. The only places mentioned are those where people gather together—the streets, markets and taverns—though exception must be made of the lonely prison cell in which a good deal of his short and mischievous life was spent, and which he hated, not so much because it was prison, place of starvation and torture though it was, but because it removed him from the multifarious society of the capital. Imprisonment is exile, he complains, and prison walls are a bandage over the eyes. The poetry of Villon is, in short, an intimate 'journal', as personal as any poetry has ever been.

*

François Villon was born in Paris towards the end of the Hundred Years' War, in 1431, the very year when Joan of Arc was burnt at the stake. An epic and glorious period in the history of France from some points of view, with the re-entry of the French king into his capital after nearly twenty years' occupation by the English, it was also from the point of view of living conditions one of the most wretched periods her people have known, a period of famine, epidemics and pestilence, a period bright with hope for the future yet dogged by the aftermath of war. Despair and cynicism reigned in the hearts of the people, who for four successive generations had known nothing but war and all it entails.

No detailed information has survived concerning Villon's earliest years, but they cannot have been particularly happy. However, he was more fortunate than many, for, son of poor parents though he was, he received the finest education available in his day. A register of the Faculty of Arts of the University of Paris reveals that François de Montcorbier—such was his original name—was awarded his *baccalauréat* in 1449 and that three years later he became, first *licencié*, then *maistre-ès-arts*. As promising a career as the age could offer lay ahead of him, possibly in the Church, or in the law-courts. He owed these early successes to the chaplain of Saint-Benoît-le-Bientourné (a church in the old Latin Quarter), Guillaume de Villon, who adopted him and from whom he took his name.

The next documents to have come down to us have a very different story to relate: in 1455 'François de Montcorbier, maistre-ès-arts' killed a priest in a quarrel, pleaded self-defence, and was granted letters of pardon. This incident threatened to put a swift end to his career at the very outset, and he clearly realised this, for he fled from Paris before hearing of his acquittal. We might expect to find him settling down after such a harrowing experience, thankful to be still alive and at liberty, but we learn that the very next year he took part in a robbery. He again left the capital, and spent a period of four years wandering about the provinces, ending up in jail at Meung-sur-Loire for some reason unknown to us. Released in 1461, when the young King Louis XI passed through the town shortly after his coronation and granted prisoners there an amnesty, back he went to Paris, soon to find himself behind bars once again. Guy Tabarie, the least important, but also the least discreet member of the gang which robbed the Collège de Navarre, had talked too freely in the congenial atmosphere of the taverns, and the whole story of Villon's part in the robbery became known to the authorities. He was freed after making a promise to restore his share of the stolen money, but the following year he was again imprisoned, this time for his part in a street brawl. He had tried the patience of the law quite enough and was now condemned to be hanged, but his luck still held good and the sentence was commuted to one of banishment from Paris for a period of ten years. The year was 1463; Villon was thirty-two years of age. He left Paris and we hear no more of him. How his life ended is a mystery. Did the gallows catch up with him? Did he produce passion plays in Poitou as Rabelais has reported, or did he, again as Rabelais tells us, come to England and join the court? If either of these equally amazing, equally Rabelaisian tales contains any truth at all, which is highly improbable, it is the former. What these anecdotes do indicate is that already in the sixteenth century Villon's last years were a matter for legend and conjecture. The very writing by Rabelais of *two* anecdotes concerning them is significant. The true facts were not known and never have been; most of Villon's life had been a good deal more public than he could have wished, but he died at least in obscure circumstances.

One point standing out clearly is this: Villon was so often charged with crimes of one sort or another, so often imprisoned, that he cannot be considered purely and simply as the victim of adverse circumstances. He was a scion of an evil age, deeply imbued with the atmosphere of the fourteen-thirties and fourteen-forties in which he grew up, but even so he must not be allowed to shed all responsibility for what he had become. He had been brought up by a member of the Church and had been given his chance. There is accordingly no reason for us to romance over him, and to see him, as did

Swinburne, as 'a wild dove lost in the whirling snow'. Give a dog a bad name . . . but no! not even this excuse will do, for even after the robbery affair, he still had a chance. Provided with all his degrees, stepping out into the world of the fourteen-fifties, when the storm-clouds of war and famine were at last beginning to blow over, he faced a future brighter with promise than any for the preceding hundred years.

What went wrong in Villon's career? The historical documents record the facts, but do not and cannot explain why he became a criminal. The answer is given indirectly in his poetry. His first work, *Le Lais*, written shortly after the robbery and just before he fled from Paris for the second time, is a mock testament in which he makes a series of farcical bequests to acquaintances he is leaving behind him. His departure is caused, he tells us, by the cruelty of his mistress who has rejected all his advances:

> Et se j'ay prins en ma faveur
> Ces doulx regars et beaux semblans
> De tres decevante saveur
> Me trespersans jusques aux flans,
> Bien ilz ont vers moy les piez blans
> Et me faillent au grant besoing.
> Planter me fault autres complans
> Et frapper en ung autre coing. (*L* IV)

It is quite possible that he had indeed suffered some disappointment in love, but it had not weighed too heavily with him; nor can we accept this as the sole reason for his flight, since in the first place, according to the confessions made by Guy Tabarie, Villon was planning to commit another robbery in Angers and was intending to make a reconnaissance there.[1]

---

[1] No value should be attached to this story according to A. Burger ('L'Entroubli de Villon' in *Romania*, 1958, pp. 485-95), although Villon did have other reasons for visiting Angers (see Bibliography, p. 161).

Secondly, although in the opening lines of the *Lais* he expounds on the miseries which his mistress has heaped on him and declares:

> . . . je suis de joye interdit
> Et de tout plaisir dechassié, (*L* 75-6)

his tongue is in his cheek, as is made obvious by the series of burlesque legacies which follows and takes up more than two thirds of the poem. Joy is not banished from his life, far from it. Moreover he compares himself at various times to a horse, a smoked herring from Boulogne and a flue-brush. He does not mean us to shed tears over his plight, unless they be tears of laughter. No doubt about it, the young François is a jester who does not take himself any more seriously than he does those around him. He has often been compared to the Romantics of the nineteenth century, but clearly nothing in his early years invites such a comparison. Nothing could be more different from the lonely melancholy of a young Romantic poet than this extrovert who revels in gay company and reveals a thorough acquaintance with the taverns of Paris—*Le Cheval blanc*, *L'Asne royé*, *La Mulle*, *La Pomme de Pin*, etc.,— and their habitués. Life is a game for him, and he treats it with a mocking and cynical indifference to its more serious aspects.

Four years have elapsed since he completed his studies, and far from having the bit between his teeth as he describes himself, he has kicked over the traces completely. His dissolute ways may have begun when he was still a student, though it is very likely that at that time his benefactor, Guillaume de Villon, maintained some degree of control over him and was responsible for his having completed his studies. Villon later informs us that this man who was more than a father to him, rescued him from many an evil plight, and we may well believe him. Here then is the key to his downfall: a flippant character, fond of gay company, thumbing his nose at life and everything in it, with all the couldn't-care-less, pleasure-at-all-cost attitude of a post-war generation.

The *Lais* was written after his early escapades, and before the arm of the law had caught up with him. Five years later, having seen the inside of several prisons, having been starved, tortured and subjected to a variety of harsh treatments, shut up in gaol alone with his thoughts, driven to introspection, he saw himself, for the first time, with no prospects except constant poverty and a miserable death in front of him. In 1461, in hiding near Paris between one imprisonment and the next, he began work on his masterpiece, *Le Testament*. Modelled closely on the *Lais*, this too was a mock will, though in fact it came much nearer to the real thing, for, caught out as it were by his own joke, Villon really did have to envisage his death now. The complaints about his plight which open the work have nothing false about them as have the corresponding ones which introduce the *Lais*. Before he began this second and final list of legacies, Villon reflected sadly on his past and set down his thoughts as they crowded untidily through his mind: his recent imprisonment at Meung-sur-Loire, the injustice of it; a curse on the bishop who had ordered it; a blessing on the king whose passage through the town had occasioned his release; his sufferings and ill-fortune; his wasted youth; the imminence of death and its dreadful omnipotence; the ephemeral nature of all life; the empty fickleness of love. The vanity of all human things is the *motif* which gradually emerges. Gone is the devil-may-care attitude, gone are the days of the gay young spark. At length he promises to get down to the substance of his will, but, unable so it seems to check this stream of regrets, reminiscences and reflections, off he goes on another digression. Finally, having given us his own very partial view of his life and fate, a view in which there is more self-pity than self-condemnation, having explained away his own wretchedness by pointing out what a miserable thing life is—particularly that of the poor—having sunk more and more deeply into this clogging morass of fatalism, he returned somewhat half-heartedly to the theme of the *Lais*. He distributed legacies, mostly worthless, inexistent or belonging to somebody else, much as in the earlier work, but the atmosphere remained noticeably different, as we shall see presently.[1] But why, after so many sober thoughts, this quite unexpected return, or attempted return, to the vein of the *Lais*? Why jest at all when the time for laughter is decidedly over? Villon himself gives us the reason:

> Au moins sera de moi memoire,
> Telle qu'elle est d'ung bon follastre.   (*T* 1882-3)

Both in his way of life and in his early verse, he had created for himself the reputation of being a clown, a jester. He might as well stay as he is, because nothing he can do will ever change his lot. Such is his attitude, but we may suspect that in fact he is unable to cast off the jester's garb for good. The reputation for frivolity which he has earned has grown too strong for him to control, and like the broom bewitched by the sorcerer's apprentice, it will no longer obey any injunctions.

Sixteenth-century dictionaries note the use of a verb *villonner*, defined by one as follows: 'Villonner est tromper l'ung, décevoir l'aultre, abuser ceux à qui on a affaire et emporter le bien des personnes sans payer, avec emprunter sans jamais rendre, comme faisoit jadix M. Françoys Villon, duquel est venu ce terme de *villonner*.'[2] Etienne Pasquier, in

---

[1] See below, pp. 23-6
[2] Quoted from the *Dictionnaire de l'ancien français* of F. Godefroy (Paris, 1881-1902), vol. VIII, p. 244

Les Recherches de la France, explains the formation of this verb in the same way.[1] In fact this is not the whole story, since *villonner* (a variant spelling of *vilonner* based on Latin *vilis* and hence pronounced with dental rather than palatal *l*) meaning 'to insult' had existed centuries before Villon's time, and Villon's contribution was to modify the old word in meaning ('to insult'>'to deceive') and possibly pronunciation (-l-> -λ-) rather than to create an altogether new verb. On the other hand the noun *villon* appears to have been a new formation; its meaning is given as follows by Randle Cotgrave, writing in the early seventeenth century: 'A cousener, cony-catcher, cunning or wittie rogue; a nimble knave; a pleasant theefe; (for such a one was François Villon, whose death a halter suited to his life).'[2] In this same century Ménage was the first to point out that *villonner* existed long before the poet was born, but then he went on to state that ' . . . ce Poëte Villon fut ainsi appellé à cause de ses friponneries et tromperies',[3] a belief still held by some scholars in the eighteenth century, for in Massieu's *Histoire de la poësie françoise*, published in 1739, it is said that Villon was in fact a nickname 'qui en langage de ce tems-là signifioit *Fripon*'.[4] This belief is still reflected in Godefroy's nineteenth-century dictionary of medieval French, where *villon* is correctly given as meaning 'voleur adroit'; two sixteenth-century uses of the word are quoted, but then this comment is added: 'Le surnom du vieux poète parisien suffit à prouver l'ancienneté du mot *villon*.' It was of course from Guillaume de Villon that the poet drew his name, not from a noun *villon* in existence before his time, but it is not inconceivable that this lover of puns (cf. *Lais=Lai* and *legs*) found a certain piquancy in adopting the name of his

[1] pp. 1093-4 of the 1607 edition, pp. 930-1 of the 1611 edition
[2] *A Dictionarie of the French and English Tongues* (London, 1611)
[3] *Les Origines de la langue françoise* (Paris, 1650), pp. 368-9
[4] p. 249

foster-father because of its resemblance, fortuitous as it happened, to the verb *villonner*.

An anonymous work of the later fifteenth century, the *Repues Franches* ('Free Feasts') made Villon the ringleader of a band of rascals living by their wits. This same reputation lived on into the sixteenth century as is shown by the foregoing definitions of *villonner* and also by Marot's lines:

> Peu de Villons en bon sçavoir,
> Trop de Villons pour décevoir,

and from the roystering rumbustiousness of Rabelais's stories about him.

Villon was wise not to attempt to destroy the name he had made for himself in his own lifetime. Without the legacies which form the main body of the *Testament*, the tragic thoughts and reminiscences with which the work opens would lack a suitable framework or any real *raison d'être*, and might well have been forgotten and not even handed down to us. Villon is shadowed by his gaily coloured other self just as Musset is by his own sombre-cloaked double. Panurge may well be a literary descendant of Villon.[1]

Scattered throughout the *Testament* are several *ballades* and *rondeaux*, set pieces whose metrical patterns had been evolved during the fourteenth century and earlier. Some are included in the musings on life, love and death, some amongst the mock legacies. Also from Villon's pen we have about twenty short poems, mostly *ballades*, not inserted in the cadre of the *Testament*. The best reflect his serious mood: the *Épitaphe Villon* or *Ballade des Pendus* as it is often called, perhaps the most intensely dramatic of all medieval French poems, in which the blackened, withered bodies swinging on the gibbet beseech

---

[1] See D. B. Wyndham Lewis, *François Villon, A Documented Survey* (London, 1928), Appendix B, pp. 342-3.

their 'freres humains' to pray for the absolution of their sins. Drama of a different kind is provided by the *Débat du Cuer et du Corps*, a debate between Villon's instinctive desire to cling to his dissolute ways and his realisation that he could and should repent and lead a better life. Less outstanding are his verses celebrating the birth of a daughter to Charles d'Orléans, a poem in praise of France, and several written in thieves' jargon purporting to give criminals useful advice, which may be summed up, not as 'Leave your evil ways!' but 'Mind you don't get caught!' In the *Testament* occurs a reference to another work by Villon, *Le Rommant du Pet au Deable*, which he bequeaths to Guillaume de Villon. This *roman* has not survived, and the reference indicates that it may never have got beyond the stage of a first draft (*T* LXXXVIII).[1] Altogether Villon has left us a little more than 3,000 lines, most of them of the short, octosyllabic pattern. It is a very small output indeed, not very much larger than a single play of Molière or Racine if the difference in length of line is taken into account. His complete works are contained in one very slender volume.

*

It is scarcely possible to have any feeling about life which has not some reflection in Villon's poetry, scarcely possible to remain unaffected by him. Rodin was inspired to carve his statue of Villon's Belle Heaulmière, the old prostitute who contemplates with disgust her withered body and thinks back with longing to the days when she was young and beautiful. This weirdly hunched and contorted figure, with the skin hanging loose in places and the bones protruding in others is extremely expressive, but equally expressive in a radically different way is Debussy's setting to music of three of Villon's

[1] It may not even have reached the stage of a first draft according to W. H. Rice ('A Villon Hypothesis', in *French Studies*, II, 1948, pp. 348-50).

ballades, including the prayer he wrote for his mother. The pre-Raphaelite D. G. Rossetti was able to find among Villon's works delicate poems of purity and innocence and picked on them for his translations, in particular the *Ballade des Dames du Temps Jadis*; whereas the more robust Swinburne, on the lookout for stronger meat, had an 'embarras du choix', translating some ten poems in all. No matter to what side of our nature he appeals, Villon's impact is always keenly felt. There is something for everybody in this kaleidoscope of emotions. With his constant ups and downs, the moments of riotous enjoyment in tavern and brothel and those of solitary confinement in a prison cell, with his knowledge of all manner of men—Church dignitaries, the learned professors of the University, the students, the crooks who made up the underworld of the capital—with his several love affairs which all seem to have gone awry, Villon certainly had a wide and varied experience of life. This experience taught him more than did his studies, as he says himself, and he has distilled the essence of it into his verse. Like all men of genius, he defies analysis in the last resort, but the three important formative factors were his character, his experiences and the atmosphere of the period. Had he lived quietly and respectably like his foster-father, Guillaume de Villon, he might never have set pen to paper. Had he lived a century later, in the brighter age of the Pléiade, he would never have written so bitterly on the vanity of human affairs. For all its success in the future, and although, as will be seen later, it anticipates certain aspects of later ages, his poetry belonged, in its very essence, to the past.

Villon remained astonishingly alive in the hearts of men. Marot, some seventy years after the composition of the *Testament*, encountered several old people still able to recite passages from it by heart. Something about him caught the popular fancy, perhaps the strange alliance of picturesque roguery and poetic genius. He is the apotheosis of the sharp-tongued wit so common amongst the people of Paris. He was the jester not of the court but of the street and tavern. He belonged to the people, whose joys and miseries he personified.

The reputation of his works has known countless vicissitudes, like the poet himself in life. His poetry has been scorned and reviled by idealistic, morally-inclined ages, but at least it has constantly given rise to statements and discussions of all kinds, and has not known that most cruel of all fates which befell even Ronsard's works for a period: utter indifference and oblivion.

CHAPTER I

Le Bien Renommé Villon

THE first printed edition of Villon's works appeared in 1489, less than twenty years after the introduction of printing in France. Nine of his poems were included in the first printed anthology of French literature, published towards 1501.[1] In 1533 his works were re-edited at the request of François I by Clément Marot, who made Villon the object of one of the earliest pieces of textual criticism in France. He had found Villon's poetry in a bad state—indeed numerous faults in the 1489 edition made nonsense of many passages—and quoted an extract to show how he emended the text and to explain the method he followed in his edition, which went through several reprints up to 1542. Only the seventeenth century saw no new edition of Villon's poetry. One of the first members of the French Academy, Guillaume Colletet, writing towards 1650, complained that Villon's works had become very hard to obtain. Other remarks he makes show that Villon's reputation as a jester had suffered no appreciable modification since the sixteenth century. The two words which come most readily to his pen when he describes Villon's poetry are *raillerie* and *naïveté*. He would number his works amongst those to which one may turn for pleasant relaxation after a period of serious study. Villon, he remarks somewhat quaintly,

---

[1] *Le Jardin de plaisance et Fleur de rhétorique.* A facsimile has been edited for the S.A.T.F. by E. Droz and A. Piaget, 2 vols. (Paris, 1910-24).

had a good knowledge of history and had the merit of being a patriot, but unfortunately poverty prevented him from acting like a man of honour and courage.[1] This last remark—how revealing it is of the seventeenth-century outlook, with its measuring of Villon according to the standards of the *gentilhomme* of Colletet's day—is the only one he has to make on Villon's serious verse. His appreciation is essentially that of a man of letters who has chanced across something rather amusing, and it is clear that from the middle of the sixteenth century onwards, once the Pléiade had become established, Villon was no longer as popular as he had been in Marot's day, but his name was remembered, and his poetry still read, at least by a restricted circle.

Some twenty years after Colletet wrote his essay, Boileau, in his *Art Poétique*, made Villon the virtual founder of modern French literature:

> Villon sut le premier, dans ces siècles grossiers,
> Débrouiller l'art confus de nos vieux romanciers.

This somewhat enigmatic reference to Villon's unravelling the confused art of the old writers of romance has been taken as proof that Boileau had never read Villon, but knew him by hearsay only. In fact, it is said, his learned friend Patru happened to mention Villon's merits to him, and he relied on these remarks for this couplet. But this is pure conjecture. If we place the couplet back in its context, we see that Boileau has just been referring to such things as harmony, cadence, choice of sounds. Poetry, he maintains, must please the ear:

> N'offrez rien au lecteur que ce qui peut plaire.
> Ayez pour la cadence une oreille sévère:
> Que toujours dans vos vers le sens, coupant les mots,

---

[1] *Vie de François Villon* reprinted in P. L. Jacob's edition of Villon's works (Paris, 1854), pp. xvii-xxxvii.

Suspende l'hémistiche, en marque le repos.
Gardez qu'une voyelle à courir trop hâtée
Ne soit d'une voyelle en son chemin heurtée.
Il est un heureux choix de mots harmonieux.
Fuyez des mauvais sons le concours odieux:
Le vers le mieux rempli, la plus noble pensée,
Ne peut plaire à l'esprit quand l'oreille est blessée.
Durant les premiers ans du Parnasse françois,
Le caprice tout seul faisait toutes les lois.
La rime, au bout des mots, assemblés sans mesure,
Tenait lieu d'ornements, de nombre et de césure.
Villon sut le premier . . .

It can reasonably be argued that, although Villon was most certainly not the inventor of caesura and such devices as Boileau seems to imagine, his lines do indeed have a more harmonious sound, and fall better on the ear, than those of his predecessors and contemporaries. In the *Ballade des Dames du Temps Jadis*, for example, and in others of his poems, there is 'un heureux choix de mots harmonieux'.[1] Moreover, his verse is free from the allegory so beloved of the medieval poet and which characterises many a medieval romance. So many writers have remarked at various times on the modernity of Villon, quite independently of Boileau's couplet, and it is very possible that for Boileau as for them, Villon was medieval in choice of themes and in outlook, but modern in style and choice of expression and in his direct approach, not cloaked by allegory and courtly convention. Boileau's statement is a sweeping one admittedly, and is inaccurate in several details, but it is not particularly wide of the mark. His dismissal of the rest of medieval literature is the result of a prejudice common to most of the seventeenth century, but if we today were allowed to read only one pre-Renaissance poet, most people would still choose Villon.

[1] See below, chap. III

The only eminent writer of the seventeenth century who may have read Villon, apart from Boileau, was La Fontaine, who counted Guillaume Colletet amongst his acquaintances; but at the best his knowledge of Villon was a casual one, as P. A. Wadsworth tells us in his book, *Young La Fontaine*: 'If he seems to resemble Villon at times—in language, in the choice of certain genres, in intimacy, in flashes of sarcastic humor—this comes about primarily from the intervention of a third party, Marot, who belongs to Villon's lineage and is one of La Fontaine's most cherished teachers.'[1] We cannot really agree with Gaston Paris when he states that there was a renewed interest in Villon at this period due to the cult of 'le naturel'; it would be more accurate to state that a small survival lingered on from that great reputation of the past, now limited entirely to men of letters. Towards the end of the century, however, in 1692, Fontenelle chose several of Villon's poems to open his *Recueil des plus belles pièces des poëtes françois*. His brief introduction has nothing of interest to say about Villon (his 'gayeté naturelle' is stressed), but the choice of poems is significant, for it gives pride of place to the lyric verse and does not differ greatly from the selection offered in modern anthologies.

In the eighteenth century Villon's name was kept alive, at least in literary circles, for his poetry was re-edited in 1723 by the Jesuit, Père Du Cerceau, who wrote a long essay in praise of Villon. This edition, based on that of Marot, must have had some success, since it was reprinted in 1742. Du Cerceau makes Villon the inventor of the 'style marotique', which, he affirms, Marot merely copied from his 'premier Maître', Villon.[2] Du Cerceau is the first critic of modern times to have ranged over the whole of Villon's verse, and he has certainly

---

[1] (Evanston, Illinois, 1952), p. 90
[2] See p. 2 of Du Cerceau's essay at the back of the 1723 edition

been captivated by it, for he attacks its disparagers, also those whose praise had only been lukewarm or who had neglected Villon in their histories of literature. He is at pains to show that the poet's real name is indeed Villon, and not, as Fauchet had stated at the end of the sixteenth century, Corbueil.[1] Fauchet had in fact been misled by the faulty text of a manuscript in his possession:

> Je suis François, dont ce me poise,
> Nommé Corbueil en mon surnom . . .[2]

This hare started by Fauchet had a long run, for his remarks on the subject were reproduced by Ménage in the seventeenth century in his *Origines de la langue françoise*,[3] and even in the following century it was still believed that Corbueil was the poet's true name, hence Du Cerceau's insistence in this matter. Du Cerceau also sets out to reconstruct a life of Villon, which, considering the scanty information available at that time, is amazingly complete, though inaccuracies inevitably occur. It is quite obvious that he had read the poetry very attentively, and he makes clear his belief that it should be known to a much wider circle of readers. The lines on poverty and wasted youth he praises for their beauty, and he cannot, he declares, refrain from quoting them.[4] The *Épitaphe Villon* he calls 'une exhortation chrétienne et touchante'.[5] He has also been struck

---

[1] *Origines des chevaliers*, pp. 509a and b of the collected edition (Paris, 1610)

[2] This MS. (F) is now in the Royal Library in Stockholm. A facsimile was published by M. Schwob in 1905. The poem referred to by Fauchet appears at the top of 67 ro. and has been added in a later handwriting. See E. F. Chaney, *François Villon according to the Stockholm MS.* (Oxford, 1943), p. 88. Corbueil may well be a corruption of *Montcorbier:* see A. Longnon, 'F. Villon et ses légataires', *Romania*, 1873, p. 207.

[3] Despite the fact that Colletet had corrected Fauchet before the appearance of Ménage's work; see *Vie de François Villon*, reprinted in P. L. Jacob's edition of Villon's works (Paris, 1854), pp. xxxiii-xxxiv).

[4] op. cit., p. 29   [5] p. 41

by the naturalness and spontaneity of Villon's poetry, and numbers of his pronouncements call for little or no modification today, as for example the following: 'Tout y coule de source, et est manié avec un badinage fin et spirituel soutenu par des expressions vives et enjoüées qui réveillent le Lecteur et lui donnent de l'esprit à lui-même.'[1] He makes particularly frequent use of the words *badin* and *plaisant* to characterise Villon, revealing that he too, despite a broader approach than that of earlier critics, thought of him above all as the jester.

The essential change that has come about since Du Cerceau wrote his essay is that for most people nowadays Villon is mainly the author of the lyric regrets and the verses on death. For this eighteenth-century enthusiast, however, Villon remains above all what he had been in the sixteenth century, the 'bon follastre', the satirical poet, though the more serious side of his verse receives greater attention than hitherto.

Du Cerceau is not the only writer of his day to find merit in Villon, but the century as a whole showed little interest in him. However, two references in Massieu's *Histoire de la Poësie Françoise* indicate that his name at least was fairly well known. Marot's couplet, quoted above: 'Peu de Villons en bon sçavoir . . .' is referred to as 'ces deux vers que tout le monde sçait',[2] and we are told that 'selon l'opinion la plus générale' Villon was 'le Héros de la vieille Poësie',[3] a remark inspired possibly by Boileau's couplet. Massieu's own remarks on Villon are less original than those of Du Cerceau, but it is noteworthy that he too makes Villon the inventor of that *badinage* usually associated with Marot. Only in the eighteen-thirties did Villon begin to be more widely known once more, but even so the reputation he held amongst the Romantics was a very dubious one. Sainte-Beuve's statement that he was 'très-apprécié des Romantiques' has been shown to have been

[1] p. 55   [2] op. cit., p. 273   [3] p. 249

the result of a misunderstanding,[1] although the Romantics had a good opportunity of knowing his poetry, since a new edition appeared in 1832, to be followed by at least three more later in the century. One feels that Villon was just the sort of figure to interest the Romantics, with their love of colour and exaltation of the picaresque. The fact is that he was too grubby a ruffian for most nineteenth-century poets and critics; he insisted too much on his poverty and degradation for their liking; he smelt too much of rags and the gutter. The sweeter-smelling Charles d'Orléans was preferred by many, for he appealed to their imagination without offending their morals. Most nineteenth-century pronouncements on Villon are bound up largely with moral questions, and consent at the most to find one or two pearls in the dungheap, to use the image applied to Villon's poetry by Sainte-Beuve and also by Théophile Gautier. Gautier was the author of what has been termed the most important commentary to have appeared on Villon before 1873, the date of the discovery of various documents in the archives of Paris which revealed a very different Villon from the one known hitherto. In his *Les Grotesques*—the very title is significant—Gautier paints a sympathetic portrait of Villon, but treats him as a second-rate poet, author of several curiosities deserving attention. Although he found Boileau's lines on Villon 'assez ridicules', Gautier none the less had a fair amount of praise for Villon and some very pertinent and penetrating comments on his verse: 'Villon fut le plus grand poète de son temps; et maintenant, après tant d'années, tant de changements dans les mœurs et dans le style,

[1] See N. Edelman, 'La Vogue de François Villon en France de 1828 à 1873' in *Revue d'histoire littéraire de la France*, 43 (1936), pp. 211-23, 321-9. In his *William Shakespeare*, Hugo gives a list of ninety-six great poets of the world, but does not include Villon (see T. Walton, 'Victor Hugo and Villon' in *Modern Language Review*, 33 (1938), pp. 50-1). It is also worthy of note that Hugo's *Notre-Dame de Paris*, though set in the reign of Louis XI, makes no mention of Villon, and neither does the *Légende des Siècles*.

sous les vieux mots, sous les vers mal scandés, à travers les tournures barbares, on voit reluire le poète comme un soleil dans un nuage, comme une ancienne peinture dont on enlève le vernis.'[1] He cannot be blamed for taking literally Villon's seemingly charitable reference to three poor, destitute orphans, which has since been shown to be a sarcastic dig at three well-known and extremely rich money-lenders of fifteenth-century Paris. Gautier deserves credit for his attitude towards the Grosse Margot *ballade*, which he dare not quote, but which he at least does not condemn outright on moral grounds, and whose qualities he has well appreciated: 'Cette ballade, il m'est impossible de la transcrire; le cant et la décence de la langue française moderne repoussent les libertés et les franches allures de sa vieille sœur gauloise. C'est grand dommage: jamais plus hardi tableau ne fut tracé par une main plus hardie; la touche est ferme, accentuée; le dessin franc et chaud; ni exagération ni fausse couleur, le mot sous la chose, c'est une traduction littérale....'[2] Gautier may have popularised Villon to some extent, but in deference to the tastes and outlook of his age he was careful not to exalt him, emphasising above all his interest as a medieval curio, a piece of flamboyant Gothic art. He would never have given Villon a place in the front rank of French poets, any more than would others of the Romantic school. None the less his remarks created quite a stir, arousing a considerable amount of polemic amongst his contemporaries, and probably inspiring his friend Gérard de Nerval to write his dramatic sketch *Villon l'Écolier*, the text of which has been lost.

A parallel has often been drawn between Villon and the Romantics, but his evolution was the very reverse of theirs, for whereas the romanticism of the nineteenth-century poet

[1] *Les Grotesques*, 1844, p. 10
[2] op. cit., p. 43

was usually one of adolescence, modified or cast off altogether in mature years:

Le temps n'est plus où j'écoute mon cœur
Se plaindre et soupirer comme une faible femme . . . (Lamartine)

Villon begins as a hard-headed, down-to-earth *farceur*; his life and experiences lead him gradually to the great lyric themes. This contrast in evolution explains the fundamental difference between the Romantics and Villon: the lack of a maudlin sentimentality in the latter, the harder, keener edge to all that he wrote, a Romanticism without dreams or rhetoric or wistful aspirations, a Romanticism where the picaresque is a way of life, a necessity, not just an affectation, not just an act put on to illustrate a literary theory on grotesqueness.

In the first two thirds of the nineteenth century, no writer of the first rank had unstinted praise for Villon, but there was a steadily increasing interest in him, revealed mainly in the histories of literature and in new editions of his work. The importance of this period in Villon studies is shown by the fact that the operative word to characterise his poetry was no longer *raillerie* but *humanité*, as is shown in an essay written by Montaiglon in 1861: 'Tous sont, avec raison, unanimes à reconnaître l'originalité, la valeur aisée et puissante, la force et l'*humanité* de la poésie de Villon.'[1]

Numbers of writers were concerned with Villon in this period extending to 1873, and only some of the more outstanding names have been mentioned here. The general trend was for the attitude towards him to become more favourable and freer from purely moral considerations as time went on, although earlier prejudices were slow to disappear, and some works still contained pronouncements such as the following: '. . . malgré le mérite réel de Villon, malgré le progrès qu'il

[1] 'Notice sur François Villon' in *Les Poètes français*, ed. E. Crépet, vol. I (1861), pp. 447-55

fit faire à la langue poétique du XVe siècle, il nous semble ...
que le poète dont la vie et les récits outragent également la
morale et la religion, et dont le cynisme s'égaie aux dépens
de tout ce qu'il y a de sacré sur terre, ne doit point être offert,
sans de sévères restrictions, aux hommages de la postérité.'[1]
Evidently the storm which Villon aroused during his lifetime
and which culminated in his banishment from Paris has had
long repercussions down the centuries.

In 1873 a new era in Villon studies was ushered in, when the
scholars Auguste Longnon and Auguste Vitu published, independently of each other, the results of their research into
the history of Villon's life and times. The first reliable edition
of Villon's poetry is also the work of Longnon. His work
was developed by Marcel Schwob and a little later by Longnon's
former pupil, Pierre Champion. The very nature of their
work in the archives made these scholars concentrate on the
life of Villon and his associates. He was revealed as a much
more complex and mysterious individual than had hitherto
been believed. Marcel Schwob refers to 'cette vie si mystéri-
eusement compliquée'[2] and stresses the difficulties of grasping
the true meaning of Villon's poetry.[3] According to Louis
Cons, Schwob made something of a mystical cult out of his
pursuit of 'un Villon étrange, compliqué, moderne d'une
modernité fin XIXe siècle'.[4] When Pierre Champion wrote
the concluding and crowning work of the archivist school in
the year 1913, his final words were: 'Villon demeure pour
nous une énigme. Nous ne pouvons le comprendre, lui et tant
d'autres esprits de son temps, aussi pervers que candides.'[5]

---

[1] D. Bonnefon, *Les Écrivains célèbres de la France.* 9th ed. n.d. (Paris), p. 43
[2] *Spicilège* (Paris, 1896), p. 6
[3] M. Schwob, *Mélanges d'histoire littéraire et de linguistique* (Paris, 1928),
p. 135. (Posthumous publication)
[4] L. Cons, *État présent des études sur Villon* (Paris, 1936), p. 66
[5] *François Villon, sa vie et son temps* (Paris, 1913, 2nd ed., 1933), vol. II,
p. 287

One can only wonder at the extreme modesty and restraint shown by the author of this erudite, richly detailed study of Villon and his times.

The information at last made available on the life of Villon, and this new aura of magic and mystery surrounding his name, created in large measure by those very scholars who had cleared up so many obscurities, led to the building-up of a Villon legend. Only Robert Louis Stevenson seems to have reacted unfavourably to the revelation that Villon had frequently been in trouble with the law. His cheaply moralising judgments represent the death-throes of the nineteenth-century prim and puritanical outlook on Villon. Stevenson really lets himself go: Villon's verse on poverty constituted 'a calumny on the noble army of the poor', the *Regrets de la Belle Heaulmière* 'an almost maudlin whimper'; in his lines on death he is 'like a man cutting capers to a funeral march', and as for the Grosse Margot poem '. . . that ballad stands forth in flaring reality, gross and ghastly, as a thing written in a contraction of disgust'.[1]

Reactions in France were very different. Théodore de Banville wrote his *Trente-six Ballades Joyeuses . . . composées à la manière de François Villon*, concluding with the following *Dizain à Villon*, dated 31 juin [*sic*] 1873, the very year when the historical documents relating to Villon's life were brought to light:

> Sage Villon, dont la mémoire fut
> Navrée, hélas! comme une Iphigénie,
> Tant de menteurs s'étant mis à l'affût,
> Dans ta légende absurde, moi je nie
> Tout, grand aïeul, hors ton libre génie.
> O vagabond dormant sous le ciel bleu,

---

[1] 'François Villon, Student, Poet and Housebreaker' in *Familiar Studies of Men and Books* (London, 7th ed., 1892), pp. 192-235

Qui vins un jour nous apporter le feu
Dans ta prunelle encore épouvantée,
Ce vol hardi, tu ne l'as fait qu'à Dieu:
Tu fus larron, mais comme Prométhée.

Banville, obviously enough, was an ardent apologist of Villon, and he was by no means alone. In the following year Huysmans apostrophised Villon in his turn, drawing like so many others before and after him the contrast between the ugliness of his life and the beauty of his poetry: 'Oh! tu es seul et bien seul! Meurs donc, larron, crève donc dans ta fosse, souteneur de gouges; tu n'en seras pas moins immortel, poète grandiosement fangeux, ciseleur inimitable du vers, joaillier nonpareil de la ballade!'[1] Jean Richepin, in his *La Chanson des Gueux* (1876), enthusiastically followed the more seamy side of Villon's poetry. Written, much of it, in argot reminiscent of the 'jargon' in which certain of Villon's *ballades* were composed, this work earned its author a month in gaol and a stiff fine. In this same year Swinburne, emulating Rossetti, whose translations of three of Villon's poems had been published as early as 1870, began his translations of ten of Villon's poems, including the *Regrets de la Belle Heaulmière*. He also composed an extremely romantic and idealising ballad in praise of Villon:

Bird of the bitter bright grey golden morn
Scarce risen upon the dusk of dolorous years,
First of us all and sweetest singer born
Whose far shrill note the world of new men hears
Cleave the cold shuddering shade as twilight clears;
When song new-born put off the old world's attire
And felt its tune on her changed lips expire,
Writ foremost on the roll of them that came
Fresh girt for service of the latter lyre,
Villon, our sad, bad glad mad brother's name! ...

[1] *Le Drageoir à épices* (Paris, 1874), p. 84

12

This somewhat febrile enthusiasm was shared by John Payne, who outdid Swinburne by translating all Villon's poetry, and added a nice crowning touch by founding the Villon Society. Under the auspices of this same society he translated, amongst other works, *The Thousand and One Nights* and the *Decameron*, a surprising combination which shows in what romantic light Villon was conceived. In the eighteen-eighties and eighteen-nineties, Verlaine, 'pauvre Lélian', was to add his quota to the legend of 'pauvre Villon'.[1]

In the early years of the twentieth century the novelist H. de Vere Stacpoole wrote a work on Villon's life and poetry, some of which he translated in his turn, D. B. Wyndham Lewis produced an extremely vivid and imaginative account of the poet and his times (see Bibliography, p. 159), and novels with a romanticised Villon as hero appeared on both sides of the Channel.[2] It is remarkable that the cult of Villon should have flourished as much in England as in France, and may even be said to have begun earlier on this side of the Channel with the series of articles by H. F. Cary in the *London Magazine* of 1821. The romantic story of his life, and the truly lyrical nature of his poetry, perhaps explain why English people have taken him to their hearts. So many translations into English, either of individual poems, or of his complete works, have appeared since those of Rossetti and Swinburne, that it is doubtful whether any other French poet can boast of as much success in this country. There is still no sign of a waning of this popularity, for at least three complete translations have appeared since the Second World War.

Meantime, scholarly editions of his poetry have continued to appear in France. That by Longnon was revised and re-

---

[1] See Y.-G. Le Dantec's edition of Verlaine's poems in the *Bibliothèque de la Pléiade* series, note on p. 997.

[2] By F. Carco, P. d'Alheim, J. Erskine, J. Huntly MacCarthy, etc.

edited several times by Lucien Foulet for the *Classiques français du Moyen Âge* series, and much useful information on the text was given by Louis Thuasne's richly annotated version, despite his rather prolix and at times unsound commentaries. However, notwithstanding the impressive array of scholarship in the early twentieth century, the definitive edition of Villon's poetry has yet to appear, and its preparation will present a formidable challenge to specialists in the field of medieval literature, who have treated many diverse aspects of his poetry in the learned periodicals and reviews. Scarcely a year has passed this century without something being written on him. He is now very different from the second-rate curiosity who headed Gautier's *Les Grotesques*.

From 1873 to 1933, the date of the second and final edition of Pierre Champion's monumental *François Villon, sa vie et son temps*, Villon was looked upon as a romantic, complex individual. He was presented as a sentimental, emotional being, constantly torn between tears and laughter. All would have agreed with the judgment passed on him by Gaston Paris at the beginning of the century in the work which he wrote in the *Grands Écrivains français* series. His outstanding characteristic according to Gaston Paris is '. . . la facilité avec laquelle il passe d'un ton à l'autre, entremêlant sans cesse le plaisant au sérieux, allant du rire aux larmes avec une brusquerie apparente qui sans doute est chez lui surtout instinctive, mais qu'il a certainement dirigée avec intention pour produire un effet artistique . . .'.[1] He was painted in bright, at times lurid, colours, all the more as he remained an enigma, a mysterious figure about whom just enough was known to foster an atmosphere of romance. He touched off all manner of creations. To Rodin's statue, Debussy's music and Swinburne's translations was added the bric-à-brac of the twentieth century:

[1] *Villon* (Paris, 1901), pp. 153-4

14

several novels, a musical comedy, a psycho-analytic study which revealed that Villon suffered from, of all things, schizophrenia. Interpretations were highly subjective, and there were as many Villons as there were poets, novelists and critics. The complications were not all in Villon.

In the year 1934 a new voice was heard: 'Quelle histoire simple, au fond, que celle de Villon!'[1] The preceding generation of scholars would certainly not have echoed this cry of the Italian scholar, Italo Siciliano, according to whom the 'tears and laughter' interpretation is nonsense. The sentimental verse with which the *Testament* opens, embodying Villon's regrets and repentance, was written in old age according to Siciliano, and added as an introduction to the burlesque legacies which had been composed originally when Villon was still young. His aim was to present the work as a sort of personal anthology, or poetical memoirs. This twentieth-century rationalisation of Villon's work gives a radically different conception of it. Where are the complications, asks Siciliano, and why speak about the poet's double nature? It is more a matter of youth and old age than of complexity of character. Moreover, there was nothing new or original about Villon. Everything he said had been said before, but his art was greater than that of his predecessors. He was a great poet and they were not. That was the only difference. Siciliano reaffirmed his beliefs in an article published in 1939.[2]

Nearer the present day an American scholar, Mrs Grace Frank, has reached conclusions basically similar to those of Siciliano, despite numerous differences on the surface.[3] Although she rejects the idea that the *Testament* is in fact a

[1] I. Siciliano, *François Villon et les thèmes poétiques du Moyen Âge* (Paris, 1934), p. 457

[2] 'Sur le *Testament* de François Villon', *Romania*, 1939, pp. 39-90

[3] 'The Impenitence of Villon' in *Romanic Review* (October 1946), pp. 225-36

fusion of two different works written at widely separated periods, Mrs Frank also finds Villon's poetry relatively simple, because even those parts of the *Testament* which are usually considered sentimental and inspired by profound repentance, in actual fact give no signs of true penitence according to her. She therefore finds in the *Testament* an 'essential psychological unity'; for her too there is no 'tears and laughter' mixture, and there are no contradictions, no complexities.

Today Villon has lost none of his greatness as a poet, although he has become a much simpler figure, easier to understand than in the early years of the century. This does not in fact spell complete rupture with the archivist school, for not only do their discoveries remain indispensable, as all would agree, but also, in the foreword to the second edition of his work, Pierre Champion seemed to foreshadow this change of attitude when he wrote: 'Si j'avais à récrire ces deux volumes, c'est vers la simplicité que je tendrais toujours. . . . Toujours plus de simplicité, c'est la règle de l'art que l'on découvre avec la vie.'[1]

The change of outlook was accompanied by a change of method, for Siciliano approached Villon first and foremost through literature. He gives us a fascinating, richly detailed survey of the various themes current throughout the medieval poetry of France, and shows how Villon made use of them. No longer is it a matter of what Marcel Schwob termed, rather optimistically perhaps, '. . . l'étude d'un texte littéraire au moyen de documents d'archives'.[2] Siciliano's broader though still basically historical approach led him to a very different Villon. The poet's erstwhile giant stature was a mere shadow; there was in fact nothing larger than life about him. He was first and foremost a man who lived in much the same way as others of his times, who wrote on the same

[1] op. cit., vol. I, p. xviii   [2] op. cit., p. 284

themes as other poets, but who was endowed with greater sensibility and a greater art.

In his demolition of the complicated structures erected by his predecessors, in his dismissal of their neo-romantic interpretations, in his insistence on a more realistic approach, the Italian scholar deserves every sympathy. Some such reaction was almost bound to come about eventually. Yet, when this has been admitted, one may be left with the impression that both Siciliano and Grace Frank have erred on the side of excessive simplicity, and that the pendulum has swung too far, as so often happens. The real Villon is more likely to be found between the two extremes. He was not the mysterious character, larger-than-life, in whom people believed at the beginning of the century. But on the other hand, the mid twentieth-century view is altogether too down-to-earth; stripped of all his glamour, Villon is now a very ordinary fellow who surprisingly enough still manages to write with consummate art—nobody denies him that—although his verse is graced by nothing original. Perhaps this new Villon is not so simple after all, for it is hard to see how so insignificant a figure ever came to write great poetry, and he still remains something of a contradiction, an *homo duplex* every bit as enigmatic as a Baudelaire or a Verlaine.

We have travelled full circle, and in the process vindicated Robert Louis Stevenson, at least in part when, following Grace Frank, we see only impenitence and cynicism in Villon's lyric verse. By all means let us strip him of the romantic interpretations of the too credulous and imaginative critic. But let not realism, with its no doubt justifiable passion for decrying the excesses of past scholarship, go so far as to make mockery of everything.

Nineteenth-century prejudices and the neo-romanticism of the early twentieth century have disappeared, but the last word has still not been said on Villon. In all probability it never will be said, since each generation will find something of itself in Villon and will interpret for itself and in its own way this most elusive of poets. What is certain is that the views of the two scholars which have been outlined above are in several ways unconvincing and call for some discussion, since both are too concerned with justifying a hypothesis whose ultimate basis is a personal impression, and are not sufficiently closely related to the poetry itself. Throughout the ages this most subjective of poetry has awakened a subjective response in its readers, and so much criticism of Villon is in fact an attempted justification of the critic's personal impressions.

*

There is nothing precise, nothing conclusive in the *Testament* to justify Siciliano's chopping it up into segments, ascribing some to Villon's youth, others to his old age, according to the tone and mood of each. An interpretation of this nature obviously demands irrefutable proof taken from the text itself if it is to be accepted. Siciliano has produced many arguments, but not one can be said to clinch the matter once for all.[1] The *Testament* follows the same pattern as the *Lais*. What the *Lais* was to his life in 1455 the *Testament* was to his life in 1461. Nothing stands outside the period 1461-3 from the point of view of tone and atmosphere[2]; several references can be ascribed to these years, whilst nothing definite takes us beyond 1463 to Villon's old age. We have only to read an account of Villon's life in these years to understand the *Testament*. The note of introspection which it introduces and which

---

[1] See 'The Date and Composition of Villon's *Testament*' by J. Fox, in *French Studies*, 7 (1953), pp. 310-22.
[2] See p. 318 of article quoted above

is quite absent from the *Lais* has grown out of his imprisonment, when he was shut up alone with his thoughts, forced to
take stock of himself. There are indications that the *Lais* was
written in a short period, possibly in one evening. The
Testament, a much bigger work, certainly covers a very much
longer period of time, but not fifteen years as the Italian
scholar has suggested.

For all its disjointed appearance, the introduction to the
Testament is not out of place. It serves a definite purpose which
links it closely and intimately to the burlesque part. It is an
apology for what he is and has been, it is an attempt to justify
his levity and way of life generally, it is a self-vindication,
written to satisfy himself as well as others. To the companions
of his student days, to the mixed society which frequented the
taverns of Paris, to the officials of the law-courts to whom his
name had become only too familiar, as the records they made
still show, to Guillaume de Villon, to his mother, to the
women he had loved, to his own inner self, he says in effect:
'I am not just a common jail-bird, who deserves only to be
shut away from society. I have been a victim of circumstance.
True, I had a good time when young, and should have studied
more than I did. Now it is too late for me to better myself;
I have let the chances slip away.' It is very likely that he, a
maistre-ès-arts, had been told by Thibault d'Aussigny, Guillaume
de Villon and others that he should have known better, and
he sets out to answer their charges in the *Testament*, for,
despite everything, he still believes firmly in himself. In his
own mind, though guilty of great heedlessness when young,
he was innocent of any serious misdemeanour, hence the at
times bewildering to-and-fro movement of his lyric verse,
now admitting a fault, now speaking out in his own defence,
and all the time showing that he had his feelings, that he had
his conscience like any decent person, and that he was not a

mere cut-throat indifferent to the serious aspects of life. His murder of a priest? Taxed with glossing over this crime, he would doubtless have replied: have I not in fact been granted full letters of pardon? The robbery of the Collège de Navarre? Necessity makes people take to evil, and hunger drives the wolf out of the woods, declares Villon, who sees himself as a Diomedes who had never met an Alexander. It is likely, moreover, that in his judgment this affair was pardonable since it had caused no actual suffering or misery, and the fact is that eventually, on promise of restitution, he was allowed to go unpunished. This act of clemency by a by no means lenient justice came not long after the writing of the *Testament*. It is not inconceivable that this work played a part in securing his release, which was all the more surprising as he was known to have been one of the main instigators of the theft. His foster-father must have protected him to some extent, but the image of the 'povre petit escollier' wronged by circumstance, ill, destitute and starving, which he was clever enough to send ahead of himself as harbinger to a Paris ready to charge him with the robbery as soon as he returned, was certainly calculated to help his case. But this anxiety to present himself in the best possible light does not necessarily mean that his confessions and self-vindications were false and hypocritical. It was his unshakable belief in himself that made his self-defence so convincing, and the strength of his feelings that made his lyricism what it is. In fact, Villon's lyric poetry exists on several different levels, of which this desire to justify himself and to explain why he chooses to remain 'le bon follastre' is the most obvious. It provides the starting-point of the work, but is clearly by no means the whole story. If it were, Villon would hardly be the great lyric poet he is.

Despite their seeming incoherence and irrelevance, the lyrical '*Regrets*', as Siciliano calls them, form an integral part of the *Testament*. The untidy layout offends the modern critic's logic, and he feels obliged to reduce it to a rational pattern. Indeed, Siciliano makes frequent use of expressions such as '. . . notre logique s'étant refusée à admettre . . .',[1] and he taxes Villon with lack of logic and coherence.[2] The modern sense of orderliness is often offended by medieval writers, but it is better when reading them to admit that their attitude is not ours. If we find them confused and muddle-headed, they would probably have found us dry and un-imaginative.

Villon was thirty at the time of beginning work on the *Testament*, and considered himself to be on the threshold of old age. There is no need to see any implicit contradiction in that, as does Siciliano. Expectation of life then was not what it is nowadays, and at the age of thirty he was justified in thinking that death might soon claim him, the more so as he was suffering from an illness which, though he jests about it, may well have been serious:

> Je congnois approcher ma seuf;
> Je crache, blanc comme coton,
> Jacoppins gros comme ung esteuf.
> Qu'esse a dire? que Jehanneton
> Plus ne me tient pour valeton,
> Mais pour ung viel usé roquart:
> De viel porte voix et le ton,
> Et ne suys qu'ung jeune coquart.   (*T* LXXII)

There is no need to conjecture that he must have been forty-five or more, simply because he remarks on the imminence of old age and death. Moreover, the feeling of old age has come to him abruptly and unexpectedly. Speaking of his youth he writes:

[1] *Romania*, 1939, p. 73
[2] p. 71

Il ne s'en est a pié allé
N'a cheval: helas! comment don?
Soudainement s'en est vollé
Et ne m'a laissié quelque don.   (*T* 173-6)

The poignancy of the introduction points to a glaring proximity
of harsh and bitter experience. The memory of suffering fades
with the years. This is not an old man near death, remote at
last from the struggle of life, looking back on it for the last
time. He is still very much *engagé*, and despite his fears of
death, still full of thoughts about the future: with help from
his relatives he might still get somewhere; if only he could fill
his belly he would willingly turn his fancies to love; provided
he can have his fling he will not mind having a 'decent death'.
He is thirty, ill and destitute, but still hopes for the future,
hopes for love, hopes for the return of the gay times he has
enjoyed so much. The burlesque *Testament* is something of a
challenge to his present miseries.

The whole work has the atmosphere of a real farewell to
Paris and all his associates and acquaintances there. It is a last
souvenir from the poet and jester Villon, even to the inclusion
of his best *ballades* and *rondeaux*. By 1461 it had become very
difficult for him to return to the capital on account of the
recent discovery of the robbery, and he must have felt that his
chances of settling down there were dwindling rapidly. The
sorrow is that of one who feels himself to be an exile from a
place he has loved dearly. It is not the nostalgia of old age.

Why insist on separating the serious from the jocular in
the *Testament*, why argue that these two moods at opposite
extremes simply cannot have existed in the same person at one
and the same time of life, when they do appear together,
intimately mingled, each arguing its own philosophy, in one
small, compact poem, the *Débat du Cuer et du Corps*? Siciliano
has very well foreseen this objection, but all he can say to

counter it is: 'Mais il s'agit d'un *Débat*. . . .'[1] Such debates in verse were indeed extremely conventional in Villon's day, but the theme permits of many variations. Just as Charles d'Orléans's debates between the Lover and his Heart, or between the poet's Heart and his Melancholy, reflect his temperament, precious, courtly and languid, so Villon's debate between his Heart and his Body, that is to say between his conscience and his dissolute nature, between what he ought to be and what he is, reflects his. The essence of Villon's debate is anything but conventional, and gives the lie to the belief that the young Villon, Villon the gay and sprightly, Villon the jester, cannot possibly have existed at the same time as the sad, melancholy being, full of reminiscences and regrets, preoccupied with his age, and that a period of many years must inevitably separate the two. The very nature of the *Débat* is enough to demonstrate the weakness of this theory.

Finally, the *Lais* and the farcical section of the *Testament* were, according to Siciliano, so close in time and theme as to constitute one and the same work, the latter continuing the former. A study of versification reveals close similarity between the two parts of the *Testament*—if for the sake of argument we admit the existence of two parts—but a very considerable difference separating the *Lais* from both parts of the major work, from the second quite as much as from the first.[2] The youthful exuberance of the *Lais* spills over into its rhymes, which throughout the poem are extremely rich. Almost 30 per cent of the masculine rhymes are of the 'léonines parfaites' (e.g. *Villon*: pa*villon*) and 'léonines plus-que-parfaites' (e.g. Uni*versité*: a*versité*) varieties; the corresponding figure for the *Testament* is 12 per cent with no significant difference between the first and second parts. 35.29 per cent of the feminine rhymes of the *Lais* are of the richest variety

[1] *Romania*, 1939, p. 80   [2] See below, pp. 72-3

(e.g. *grongniée*: *renfrongniée*), 18.04 per cent only of the *Testament*, again with no significant difference between the two parts of the work. On the other hand, the poorest rhymes of all—the masculine 'rimes assonantes' (e.g. bl*anc*: b*anc*) are not far from twice as common throughout the *Testament* as in the *Lais*, 15.74 per cent as against 9.89 per cent. Other considerable differences in matters of rhyme and versification all point to the unity of the *Testament* and the isolation of the *Lais*. In the earlier poem Villon deliberately pursues the longest masculine rhymes, more difficult to achieve than their feminine counterparts, whereas in the later one he is less interested in such rhyming exploits, just as he is less interested in farce purely for its own sake. What farce there is in the *Testament* is mostly very different from that of the first work, less playful, less a matter of fun and games, often concealing a sharp gibe or a nasty sting in the case of those who had earned his dislike, or a legacy revealing a far greater depth of feeling than hitherto in the case of his friends and relatives. The emphasis has gone from the words and syllables to the feelings and ideas. Here, for example, is the bequest he makes to his lady-love in the *Lais*:

> Item, a celle que j'ai dit,
> Qui si durement m'a chassié
> Que je suis de joye interdit
> Et de tout plaisir dechassié,
> Je laisse mon cuer enchassié,
> Palle, piteux, mort et transy:
> Elle m'a ce mal pourchassié,
> Mais Dieu luy en face mercy! (*L* x)

This mock tragic tone of the supposed martyr to love hardly arouses our pity. The colours are laid on far too thickly, and it is obvious that we are not meant to take any of this too seriously, even though there is no reason to doubt that Villon has indeed been crossed in love. In the *Testament* the tone is very different:

> Item, m'amour, ma chiere rose,
> Ne luy laisse ne cuer ne foye;
> Elle ameroit mieulx autre chose,
> Combien qu'elle ait assez monnoye.
> Quoy? une grant bource de soye,
> Plaine d'escuz, parfonde et large;
> Mais pendu soit il, qui je soye,[1]
> Qui luy laira escu ne targe.   (*T* xc)

The wry jesting of the *Lais* has given way to bitter sarcasm and hatred.

In the *Lais*, he leaves to his foster-father Guillaume de Villon his reputation, already of a kind to cause nothing but displeasure to the poor chaplain, but in the *Testament* he is far more ready to show his gratitude:

> Item, et a mon plus que pere
> Maistre Guillaume de Villon,
> Qui esté m'a plus doulx que mere
> A enfant levé de maillon:
> Degeté m'a de maint bouillon,
> Et de cestuy pas ne s'esjoye,
> Si luy requier a genouillon
> Qu'il m'en laisse toute la joye.   (*T* LXXXVII)

Just how Guillaume would have received the *Rommant du Pet au Deable* bequeathed to him in the *Testament* is quite impossible to say, but his works were the only genuine kind of legacy the destitute Villon could make, as when he left to his mother the prayer addressed to the Virgin Mary.

In the *Lais* his friend Ythier Marchant receives his sword,

---

[1] For the reading 'qui je soye' and for the meaning of the expression, see F. Lecoy, 'Notes sur le texte ou l'interprétation de quelques vers du *Testament* de Villon' in *Romania*, 1959, pp. 502-3.

which he would first of all have to take out of pawn, however, but in the *Testament* he is given something of far greater value: the *rondeau* on the death of a mistress, a very moving little poem, even though it may have been intended, according to Champion, as a pastiche of the love-poetry of Charles d'Orléans and Alain Chartier:

> Mort, j'appelle de ta rigueur,
> Qui m'as ma maistresse ravie,
> Et n'es pas encore assouvie
> Se tu ne me tiens en langueur:
> Oncques puis n'eus force, vigueur;
> Mais que te nuysoit elle en vie,
>   Mort?
>
> Deux estions et n'avions qu'ung cuer;
> S'il est mort, force est que devie,
> Voire, ou que je vive sans vie
> Comme les images, par cuer,
>   Mort!   (*T* 978-89)

In the *Lais*, the hospitals receive window-frames with spiders' webs in place of glass, but in the *Testament* Villon shows greater readiness to sympathise with those who suffer:

> Item, ne sçay qu'a l'Ostel Dieu
> Donner, n'a povres hospitaulx;
> Bourdes n'ont icy temps ne lieu,
> Car povres gens ont assez maulx.   (*T* 1644-7)

Despite some superficial resemblances, the *Lais* and the *Testament* are entirely different works, separated by a period of five years and by some major, maturing experience, evidently his wanderings about the provinces, culminating in his imprisonment at Meung-sur-Loire. The *Testament* is in effect a crystallisation of the *Lais*.

*

The *Testament* has a unity, but it is not simply a matter of an unvaryingly impenitent attitude towards his misdemeanours as Grace Frank has suggested. To see only hypocrisy in every confession is absurd. Villon regrets that he had not worked harder when young, for then he would have enjoyed some comfort in later life, and there can be no reason to doubt his sorrow here; it is guaranteed by his very realisation that he has thrown away chances of making good. That he was indeed destitute is obvious enough, and that he regretted the fact is even more obvious:

> Hé! Dieu, se j'eusse estudié
> Ou temps de ma jeunesse folle
> Et a bonnes meurs dedié,
> J'eusse maison et couche molle.
> Mais quoi? je fuyoie l'escolle,
> Comme fait le mauvais enfant.
> En escripvant ceste parolle,
> A peu que le cuer ne me fent. (*T* XXVI)

Grace Frank asks: 'Are these the thoughts of a contrite sinner, as is so often held? Does a penitent pretend to be broken-hearted over playing hooky and over failure through bad behavior to earn a comfortable bed? Is Villon really weeping over his lost youth here?'[1] It is true that the rather naïve tone of this stanza may raise a smile, but this is no reason to doubt the strength of Villon's feeling. It is not simply the lack of a comfortable bed and the 'playing hooky' that occasion his grief. This is merely a symbolical way of depicting his present destitution and its causes. This use of symbolical images is a feature of Villon's poetry, as when he says of his former companions who have also fallen on evil days: '... pain ne voient qu'aux fenestres.' 'Not entirely foolish, not entirely wise',[2] he accepts some of the blame for his present miseries,

---

[1] op. cit., p. 227   [2] See below, p. 81

but not all. It must be conceded that he allows himself a generous measure of self-pity, ever ready to make excuses and to condone his own misdeeds:

> Necessité fait gens mesprendre
> Et faim saillir le loup du bois. (*T* 167-8)

but the fact that he did not see himself as others saw him is no proof of hypocrisy or of a cynically impenitent frame of mind. It only makes him all the more human.

There is so much obviously deep and genuine feeling in the *Testament*—hatred of poverty, fear of death, and so on— that to see hypocrisy in numerous lyrical passages would be to make of the work a bewildering hotch-potch of heartfelt regrets and shallow deceit, switching abruptly from one to the other just as Siciliano's version switches about from youth to old age. There is indeed a dichotomy in Villon's poetry, but its nature must not be misrepresented. He is able to make us feel the pathos of adverse circumstances, but this does not prevent him from flinging in an ironical jest about them, witness the two poems written while under sentence of death (or which purport to have been written while under sentence of death). One declares with a humour that is at once macabre and trivial that his neck will soon know the weight of his backside, whereas the other—the *Ballade des Pendus*—is one of the most moving of all lyric poems to have been written in the French language.

This same duality is revealed, as we have already seen, in the *Débat*. In the view of the American scholar, cynicism prevails in this poem, for it gives no evidence, she says, of regret or promise of reform.[1] Written shortly after the *Testament*, the *Débat* is quite fundamental to an understanding of Villon's mentality, and its very existence is enough to weaken Siciliano's

[1] op. cit., p. 229

thesis. It is necessary in connection with Grace Frank's conception of Villon to take a closer look at this *ballade*, which in
a number of respects is the keystone of all Villon's work; it
is reproduced here in its entirety:

Qu'est-ce que j'oy?—Ce suis je!—Qui?—Ton cuer,
Qui ne tient mais qu'a ung petit filet:
Force n'ay plus, substance ne liqueur,
Quant je te voy retraict ainsi seulet,
Com povre chien tapy en reculet.—
Pour quoy est-ce?—Pour ta folle plaisance.—
Que t'en chault il?—J'en ay la desplaisance.—
Laisse m'en paix!—Pour quoy?—J'y penserai.—
Quant sera ce?—Quant seray hors d'enfance.—
Plus ne t'en dis.—Et je m'en passeray.—

Que penses tu estre?—Homme de valeur.—
Tu as trente ans.—C'est l'aage d'un mulet.—
Est ce enfance?—Nennil.—C'est donc folleur
Qui te saisist?—Par ou? Par le collet?—
Rien ne congnois.—Si fais.—Quoy?—Mouche en let;
L'ung est blanc, l'autre est noir, c'est la distance.—
Est ce donc tout?—Que veulx tu que je tance?
Se n'est assez, je recommenceray.—
Tu es perdu!—J'y mettrai resistance.—
Plus ne t'en dis.—Et je m'en passeray.—

J'en ay le dueil; toy, le mal et douleur.
Se feusses ung povre ydiot et folet,
Encore eusses de t'excuser couleur:
Si n'as tu soing, tout t'est ung, bel ou let.
Ou la teste as plus dure qu'ung jalet,
Ou mieulx te plaist qu'onneur ceste meschance!
Que respondras a ceste consequence?—
J'en seray hors quant je trespasseray.—
Dieu, quel confort!—Quelle sage eloquence!—
Plus ne t'en dis.—Et je m'en passeray.—

Dont vient ce mal?—Il vient de mon maleur.
Quant Saturne me feist mon fardelet,
Ces maulx y meist, je le croy.—C'est foleur:
Son seigneur es, et te tiens son varlet.
Voy que Salmon escript en son rolet:
«Homme sage, ce dit il, a puissance
Sur planetes et sur leur influence.»—
Je n'en croy riens; tel qu'ilz m'ont fait seray.—
Que dis tu?—Dea! certes, c'est ma creance.—
Plus ne t'en dis.—Et je m'en passeray.—

Veulx tu vivre?—Dieu m'en doint la puissance!—
Il te fault . . .—Quoy?—Remors de conscience,
Lire sans fin.—En quoy lire?—En science,
Laisser les folz!—Bien j'y adviseray.—
Or le retien!—J'en ay bien souvenance.—
N'aten pas tant que tourne a desplaisance.
Plus ne t'en dis.—Et je m'en passeray.   (PD XI)[1]

Throughout the four stanzas, the Body, in its role of the jester,
does indeed remain obdurate to the earnest counsels of the
Heart, and answers its questions only in a flippant, offhand
manner, although in the last stanza it is moved to make some
sort of defence, using the argument that appears in the *Testament* as well: fate has made me what I am. In the envoi,
however, a subtle though quite definite change may be
observed: 'Do you really want to live?' This opening question
at once catches the Body's interest, for the reply, still slightly
ironical perhaps, contains an obvious foundation of truth:
'May God grant me the power to do so!' The Heart continues: 'You need . . .', and the Body interrupts in its anxiety
to know the secret: 'What?' This is the first time the Heart's

---

[1] The modifications suggested by Burger (op. cit., p. 30) have been taken
into account, but not the more extensive emendations proposed by Benedetto
(see Bibliography, p. 160).

remonstrances have not been shrugged off with a jest or a sarcastic rejoinder. The reply is 'Remorse, read unceasingly.' And how does the Body respond to this? If the bantering tone of the first four stanzas were maintained here, the mere mention of remorse would be enough to provoke a sneer: 'Remorse, why remorse? I have wronged nobody', but the reply in point of fact is: 'What should I read?' The Heart expounds: 'Read for knowledge and do not consort with fools.' 'I'll take good heed of it', is the answer, and the lack of any underlying cynicism is emphasised when the Heart insists: 'Now don't forget', and the Body meekly replies, 'I'll remember it well.' The refrain is of course still the same: 'I've nothing more to tell you.'—'And I can do without it', but the preceding lines demand that this final rejoinder by the Body be taken seriously here, without the mocking intent made obvious in the four stanzas of the poem. The advice just accepted with such meekness and resignation is sufficient, and the Heart has no need to insist any more than it has done already. What more was there to be said? We can hardly expect a reading list to be included in the remonstrances! It is worth noting, moreover, that it was part of the art of the medieval writer of *ballades* to keep the same refrain but to give it a different shade of meaning, particularly in the envoi, as Villon does here. To refer to '... the twisted irony of a man who can envisage with equanimity his evil self triumphing over the good counsels of his own conscience ...'[1] is to ignore what the poet himself says. The genius of Villon is revealed in the subtlety of this poem. It really is a debate, and does not remain static from beginning to end. The arguments intertwine and do not run parallel without ever meeting. The psychological interest is very real. It has been suggested that the *Débat* was written only to placate the authorities whose

[1] p. 235

wrath had so often been roused by Villon's unruly conduct, but this is pure conjecture, and if the theory contains any truth, it is clearly not the whole truth, for this would make of the poem a far more superficial work than it is in fact.

Even the celebrated *Épitaphe*: 'Freres humains, qui après nous vivez . . .', gives, we are told, no recognition of personal guilt.[1] But why look for signs of repentance in a poem which is so obviously not written primarily from this angle? The real point lies in its beseeching other men to pray for the absolution of these criminals left hanging on the gallows: 'Mais priez Dieu que tous nous vueille absouldre!' How can there be absolution without sin, and how can there be a request for absolution without admission of sin, of guilt? The poem is a prayer for Christian mercy, for forgiveness, and therefore a recognition of guilt, not dwelt on at length because it is not primarily the subject of the poem, but it is inherently implicit in every line, and is particularly noticeable in the second stanza:

> Se frères vous clamons, pas n'en devez
> Avoir desdaing, quoy que fusmes occis
> Par justice. Toutesfois, vous sçavez
> Que tous hommes n'ont pas bon sens rassis;
> Excusez nous, puis que sommes transsis,
> Envers le fils de la Vierge Marie,
> Que sa grace ne soit pour nous tarie,
> Nous preservant de l'infernale fouldre.
> Nous sommes mors, ame ne nous harie;
> Mais priez Dieu que tous nous vueille absouldre!
>
> (*PD* XIV, 11-20)

Similar remarks may be made about the Grosse Margot *ballade*, in which, according to this same scholar, no trace of remorse is revealed. But Villon's summing-up on his life in the brothel:

[1] pp. 229-303

Je suis paillart, la paillarde me suit.
Lequel vault mieulx? Chascun bien s'entresuit.
L'ung vault l'autre; c'est a mau rat mau chat.
Ordure amons, ordure nous assuit;
Nous deffuyons onneur, il nous deffuit,
En ce bordeau ou tenons nostre estat.   (*T* 1622-7)

clearly implies a feeling of disgust, a moral condemnation.
Could this come from an impenitent sinner, a man without a
conscience, without a sense of shame?

*

Often cynical, but not always; often a liar, but not invariably so; often guilty of sin, but, at heart, very conscious
of the fact. In the late nineteenth century the critic was the
victim of Villon's bluff. The poet was looked upon as having
been downtrodden and misunderstood, a 'wild dove lost in
the whirling snow'. Now the tables have been turned, and
the joke has rebounded.

*

Villon's poetry invites speculation on his character and life.
Was he really sincere in his lyrical verse or was he nothing but
cynical? Does he really mean what he says or is his tongue in
his cheek? Is he in fact writing this poetry at the age of thirty
or is it not rather a late revision, belonging to his old age?
Admittedly these are vital questions which have to be asked.
The works themselves invite them. But will questions of this
sort ever be answered to everybody's satisfaction? Subjective
poetry awakens a subjective response. So many different
interpretations are possible, so many different answers can be
given, that the nature of Villon changes from age to age, from
generation to generation, not merely according to new discoveries which have been made, but also according to the

33

atmosphere and outlook of each age, and, of course, the temperament of the particular writer. It seems to have been ordained that, as a punishment for his crimes, Villon must forever haunt his 'brother men' who have come after him, and must live on in perpetual torment. Already in his own lifetime there was a certain mercurial quality about him. Like a cat with several lives, this individual known variously as François de Montcorbier, François des Loges, Michel Mouton, François Villon, narrowly missed death in a fight with a priest, escaped by sheer luck from two terms of imprisonment which might easily have dragged on for years, lay in his prison cell under sentence of death and wrote his own epitaph, and yet was given his freedom again. Fate kept him dangling, ever reluctant to deal the final blow. Just as he cheated his contemporaries, so he cheats posterity, for we have no idea what became of him, nor can we be sure that we have always understood him aright. Even long after his death he still manages to undergo mysterious changes, as when for a period of over a hundred years, owing to the faulty manuscript in the possession of Claude Fauchet referred to earlier, he was known as François Corbueil. Has any other writer changed his name in this way after his death? Today even the very name Villon is being transformed, for instead of being pronounced as in *pavillon* (the rhyme *Villon: pavillon* appears in the *Lais*) the *l* is very frequently sounded as in *vilain*.[1] Indeed the most mercurial of poets!

Speculation on Villon the man is bound to continue, but there are clear signs that attention nowadays is turning more to the quality of the poetry itself. As early as 1933 Fernand Desonay wrote: '. . . peu de critiques ont envisagé Villon *sub specie artis*. La personnalité mystérieuse de l'homme les a, plus

---

[1] See 'La Prononciation du nom de Villon', by A. Langfors and A. Dauzat, in *Revue internationale d'onomastique*, vol. VI (1954), pp. 87-8.

que l'œuvre, séduits.'[1] Desonay's own chapters on the art of
Villon as a poet have some shrewd and original observations
to make. This *sub specie artis* attitude towards Villon has been
brought out more clearly by Leo Spitzer, the distinguished
exponent of stylistics. In his study of Villon's *Ballade des Dames
du Temps Jadis* he criticises the traditional approach to medieval
texts: '. . . on approche les textes littéraires du moyen âge avec
un parti-pris presque exclusivement érudit et historique, on ne
les considère pas avant tout comme œuvres d'art, mais comme
documents ou témoignages servant à des buts étrangers à la
poésie. On discutera plus volontiers la genèse et l'évolution
de ces œuvres, leurs sources et leur influence, leurs rapports
avec d'autres œuvres, l'histoire des mœurs ou de la littérature
—on décrira moins volontiers leur être, leur entité, on ré-
fléchira moins sur la qualité indestructible de cet art, sur les
raisons pourquoi, non seulement les contemporains pouvaient,
mais nous autres modernes pouvons encore les considérer
comme des incarnations éternelles de la beauté.'[2] In fact the historical approach has added very considerably to our understanding of Villon, but unless new documents are unearthed
it has had its say. Although that type of criticism based on
personal impressions and opinions will always continue,
attention is now likely to be concentrated more on the poetry
itself, not so exclusively, as in the past, on *what* Villon says,
which is open to all sorts of conjecture and controversy, but
on *how* he says it, on his style, on the aesthetic quality of his
verse. A stylistic appreciation of medieval French verse along
the lines envisaged by Spitzer appeared some years ago: P.
Guiraud's *Les Sources médiévales de la poésie formelle: la rime*
(Groningen, 1952). This is a brief but interesting study of the

[1] *Villon* (Paris, 2nd ed., 1947), p. 187
[2] 'Étude ahistorique d'un texte: *Ballade des Dames du Temps Jadis*' in
Modern Language Quarterly, vol. I (1940), p. 7.

harmony achieved by medieval poets between sounds, particularly rhymes, and meaning, but no mention is made of Villon. More relevant for our purposes is 'The Stylistic Structure of Villon's Ballades', by W. H. Rice.[1] This too is a brief study. It does not set out to survey comprehensively Villon's *ballades*, but aims only at pointing out that eleven of them follow a basic pattern, whereby generalisations in the first two stanzas lead to a 'more specific or more personal or more picturesque'[2] treatment of the theme in the third.

[1] In *Symposium*, vol. III (1949), pp. 105-13   [2] p. 106

CHAPTER II

Difficulties of the Stylistic Approach

IF Villon could return to earth and hear his poetry read aloud today, he would have difficulty in recognising it, for not only has pronunciation undergone considerable change since the fifteenth century, but also the whole conception of the reading of poetry has been transformed. The would-be critic of the stylistic qualities of medieval verse is accordingly faced with a problem at the very outset: is he to attempt a reconstruction of the original pronunciation and reading habits on which to base his observations, or is he to study the verse as it would be read and pronounced at the present day, and with the meanings which have accumulated around words which may well have been quite foreign to the original author? Leo Spitzer adopts unhesitatingly this latter solution, pointing out that since Villon's day *antan* has acquired new shades of meaning which enrich his celebrated refrain: 'Mais où sont les neiges d'antan?' just as Racine's lines:

> Ariane, ma sœur! de quel amour blessée
> Vous mourûtes aux bords où vous fûtes laissée!

have benefited from the fact that the past historic has now become archaic in speech. He sees no reason to attempt to oppose such changes, and asks: '. . . pourquoi n'inscririons-nous pas à l'avoir du poète l'apport des siècles ultérieurs?'[1]

[1] op. cit., p. 14

37

Professor Ullmann adopts the opposite point of view. Doubt-less he is right in theory when he argues that '. . . from a strictly scientific point of view, it is desirable and even im-perative to eliminate modern connotations',[1] but in practice this may well leave one with some misgivings. Just how relevant to the appreciation of literature, and especially of poetry, can 'a *strictly* scientific point of view' be? Is there, moreover, any point in restoring the original if the sole result of this academic exercise is to detract from the present value of the work? It may be in the interests of science to destroy the illusion that time has created, but it is hardly in the in-terests of literature, for the effect of eliminating all modern connotations must be to pin a work firmly down in its own age and *milieu*, whereas all literature worthy of the name should, through the very effects of time, acquire a timelessness of its own. Only the lesser works are destroyed by time; they become quaint and old-fashioned, and lose all relevance to life; the greater ones, on the other hand, modify and enrich their meaning, but always remain relevant. Time is an excellent arbiter. Thus C. Day Lewis tells us that Shakespeare's

> Rough winds do shake the darling buds of May,
> And summer's lease hath all too short a date

has gained with the passing of time, for 'lease' and 'date' were pedantic legal jargon in Shakespeare's day, but time has softened the edges of these words. He quotes Shelley's dictum that time forever develops new and wonderful applications of the truth which poetry contains.[2] This evolution is bound to occur, and restoration of the original is only imperative on those relatively few occasions when a meaning has changed for the worse and so made a travesty of the author's text. It

---

[1] *Style in the French Novel* (Cambridge, 1957), p. 21
[2] *The Poetic Image* (London, 1947), pp. 92-3

is as well to explain, for example, that when Corneille refers to women as 'le sexe imbécile' he is using this expression in its etymological sense of 'the weak sex'. In most instances (there must always be exceptions), a complete restoration is not desirable, but in any case, for texts written long ago, it is not even possible. A poem composed in a period as remote as the fifteenth century can never reveal the exact size and nature of the semantic field of any one of its words. The precise effect a word had on the ear and mind of those times is conjectural, since the flavour of the written language is conditioned largely by the contemporary spoken idiom, of which we have only scant knowledge. Doubt is made all the stronger by the fact that, despite the valiant efforts of scholars, little reliable information is possessed about the intonation of those days. Our appreciation has perforce to be, in part at least, a modern one.

Attempts to revert wholly to the original would involve many other impossibilities. We cannot, for example, mould our judgment, our tastes and outlook on those of the past. If we were to manage this for the later fifteenth and early six-teenth centuries we should find ourselves dismissing Villon and preferring lines such as these, which occur at the end of a poem by Guillaume Crétin attacking the morals of the ladies of Lyons:

> Trop me desplaist que tant lai*dure dure*;
> Luxure sur toute no*blesse blesse*.
> Homme qui voit celle lai*dure dure*
> Pro*cure cure*, la corrom*pure pure*,
> Rom*pure pure*, car la sim*plesse blesse* . . .

What strikes the modern reader about these lines is the com-plete lack of harmony between form and subject-matter. It is rather like trying to deliver an address on 'Educational Problems in the Modern World' in sentences of the 'See you later, alligator' type. What offends the ear, and the taste, of the mid-twentieth century was found quite delightful then, but the moment we protest against this, or if we simply fail to share this outlook, we are standing outside the period. It may be objected that some writers, by refusing to be slaves to literary fashion, make themselves more accessible to future generations. This cannot be claimed of Villon at least, for though he was not attracted by the complex rhyme patterns beloved of the *Grands Rhétoriqueurs*, and although he fore-shadows the future in some respects as we shall see presently, he was, in thought and outlook, very much a man of his day.[1]

What really matters is the relevance of the work to the modern outlook, for this, and this alone, will keep it alive outside purely academic circles. How the poem has stood the test of time is the crux of the matter. The question inevitably arises: are the original pronunciations, meanings, intonations, tastes, etc., to be ignored altogether? Most certainly not. The critic must do his utmost to take them into account wherever they are known and wherever they have significance, but he must not indulge in the fancy that, by so doing, he has 're-stored' the original. The most that can be achieved is a com-promise solution, and the most meticulous scholar can never get beyond that, for even were he able to restore the exact sound and significance of the original, he would never tune his ear and mind wholly to it, and still less those of his readers.

The critic concerned with the interpretation of details is constantly beset by the fear that he may be reading into the text something the author never intended, that he may be seeing effects of style where none were sought, so making himself as ridiculous as Molière's blue-stocking Philaminte when she says to Trissotin, author of some *précieux* verse:

[1] See above, p. xxii

40

Mais quand vous avez fait ce charmant *quoi qu'on die*,
Avez-vous compris, vous, toute son énergie?
Songiez-vous bien vous-même à tout ce qu'il nous dit,
Et pensiez-vous alors y mettre tant d'esprit?

However droll Philaminte's fanatical pedantry may be, she at least avoids the basic assumption so often made that an author must be fully aware of all the possible stylistic ramifications of his writing. Doubtless most stylistic features are deliberate, but some are certainly intuitive, the result of subconscious feeling rather than of reasoning, and a few are the result of sheer chance, having passed unnoticed at the time of composition, or else having been brought about by the effects of time. If such concrete matters as imagery are obviously intentional, others such as rhythm and sound patterns are not always necessarily so, and critics are sometimes divided in their attitude towards them. The accumulation of *s* sounds in Racine's:

Pour qui sont ces serpents qui sifflent sur vos têtes?

is a coincidence according to some authorities, for, they maintain, serious poets of the seventeenth century scorned amusements of this sort[1]; whilst others maintain that alliterative effects of this nature were deliberately sought after by Racine and do much to enhance the aesthetic appeal of his verse.[2] Which attitude can be deemed the more reasonable? Are features of this nature to be considered as effects of style, to be dismissed as mere chance, or must defeat be accepted and the doubt allowed to remain? The answer must surely be that in any detailed and comprehensive account, such features have

---

[1] F. Brunot and C. Bruneau, *Précis de grammaire historique de la langue française* (3rd ed., 1949), p. 589.

[2] J. Marouzeau, *Précis de stylistique française* (Paris, 3rd ed., 1950), p. 43, and M. Grammont, *Le Vers français* (Paris, 4th ed., 1937), p. 303

to be included and treated as effects of style if for no other reason than that they are there and can influence anyone who reads or hears the verse. Where the full relevance of the poem to its author and *milieu* cannot be ascertained, we can at least pronounce more clearly on the relevance it has in our own epoch. The text itself must obviously come first, along with the author's aims where these can easily be seen or elucidated, but more important ultimately than the author's aim, and certainly much clearer to the modern reader, is the effect achieved, and since words are imperfect tools at best, the two are rarely identical, particularly when the work involved was written centuries ago. If stylistics is to play a useful part in literary criticism, it must relate the work to the present as well as to the period of its composition. With texts of the distant past stylistics should not confine itself to an historical approach, but it has so far tended to do this, hence declarations of this sort: 'Personnellement, je ne pourrais, sur le détail d'un texte du moyen âge, qu'émettre des hypothèses invérifiables, et par là même de peu d'intérêt scientifique.'[1] As an example of scholarly caution this is admirable and quite unassailable, but it does little to help those who feel, reasonably enough surely, that medieval texts have a stylistic value and are still capable of interesting the modern reader. The effect of this negative attitude is to relegate medieval texts to an impenetrable past, but this is not necessary for anyone who accepts that, at least in so far as texts written several centuries ago are concerned, stylistics cannot be wholly objective or wholly scientific. Mainly objective certainly, but subjective still to some extent (complete objectiveness, however fashionable it may be—cf. abstract art, 'littérature objective' etc.—is something of a will-o'-the-wisp); scientific, but not wholly neglectful of intuition (what science can neglect intuition, besides?); dealing mainly

---

[1] C. Bruneau, 'La Stylistique' in *Romance Philology*, vol. V (1951), p. 13

with the text as it was at the time of its composition, but with present-day connotations taken into account as well. Past and present must be separated where possible, but the fact must be accepted that the demarcation line cannot always be determined with precision.

Much has been written in recent years on this subject of the appreciation of poetry of the remote past, and many warnings sounded about the danger of being too exclusively modern in our approach. Here is what Professor C. S. Lewis has to say on the subject: 'If we read an old poem with insufficient regard for change in the overtones, and even the dictionary meanings, of words since its date—if, in fact, we are content with whatever effect the words accidentally produce in our modern minds—then of course we do not read the poem the old writer intended. What we get may still be, in our opinion, a poem; but it will be our poem, not his.'[1] Although no poem should ever be read without reference of any kind to its period of composition, it is certain that we do not read Villon's poetry nowadays as he himself intended, or as his contemporaries read it. In his own eyes, and in those of the people of his day, he was, as we have seen, a clownish figure, author of some comical verse. It is not before the late seventeenth century that his more lyrical work —an aside in his own estimate—begins to receive attention. In the *Testament* he repeatedly apologises for this verse which is now so prized, and promises to get on with the real subject, the mock will (see *T* 257-8, 723-4, 777-8, 831-2). That no irony is present in his attitude here is shown by the fact that the legacies take up some two thirds of the poem. It is about a passage of his lyrical verse that Villon writes:

> Ceste matiere a tous ne plaist,
> Ennuyeuse est et desplaisante.   (*T* 267-8)

---

[1] *Studies in Words* (Cambridge, 1960), p. 3

The modern reader would apply these lines more willingly to the farcical passages of the *Testament*, whose interest is limited nowadays because of the very topical nature of many of the allusions, already incomprehensible to Clément Marot seventy years after they were written, and because this type of humour palls very quickly, for us at least, if not for Villon's contemporaries. Villon would be astonished if he could learn how his poetry is interpreted now. We may feel that we have at last got it in its true perspective, that we at last realise what Villon really wanted to say but had to limit because of circumstances of all kinds, that we moderns have succeeded in getting through to the real Villon. But what proof is there that the 'bon follastre' attitude was not in fact uppermost in his mental make-up? His way of life should not be overlooked in a consideration of this.

Attitudes change, and change fundamentally, and the meaning of a poem is not and cannot be fixed for all time the moment it is set down on paper. It is as open to different interpretations as any sonata of Beethoven. And surely, if poetry were immutable, its value would be greatly diminished. When we read a poem, particularly a lyric poem, it is bound to become in some measure our poem. In his discussion of Valéry's conception of poetry M. Jean Hytier has these extremely important observations to make: 'La complexité du poème ne peut se réduire à une suite d'affirmations. Les notions qu'il fait intervenir sont impliquées dans un jeu de relations dont l'appréciation peut varier d'un esprit à l'autre, et cela dans les poèmes les plus clairs. . . . Parler de sens d'un poème, c'est employer dans le domaine du cœur un langage fait pour la raison. . . . On embarrasserait beaucoup d'amateurs en leur demandant à brûle-pourpoint ce que signifie le *Clair de Lune* de Verlaine, alors que le souvenir de leur émotion de lecture est resté en eux vivace. L'expérience montre que, dans les poèmes où la pensée n'offre aucune difficulté d'assimilation, on a à peine fait attention à elle, et qu'on a été tout le temps bien plus occupé par les jeux de l'imagination et du sentiment et par les effets du rythme et des sonorités.'[1] M. Hytier sums up his remarks as follows: '. . . dans un poème, il y a du sens plutôt qu'un sens.' It follows that a poem's effect on the mind is akin to that of music more than to that of prose. What poetry conveys is an impression, not a meaning, unless we widen this latter term to include the whole state of mind evoked by a poem. For a multiplicity of reasons, therefore, the critic's endeavours to penetrate to the root meaning of a poem can be only partially successful, and the more remote the poem is in time, the more difficult does the task become.

The very last idea this monograph is intended to convey is that there is such a thing as the 'correct' interpretation of Villon, or that it is possible to arrive at a definitive judgment of the value of his poetry. The greatest danger in this type of criticism is that it may appear to dictate to others what their appreciation should be. The most that can be done is to point to those features susceptible of objective analysis, particularly those relating to rhythm, sound patterns, syntax and imagery. Although a synthesis based on a study of such traits may not always succeed in capturing the spirit of the work as a whole, it should not be imagined that these features are mere external ornaments cloaking the real essence of poetry. Whether or not a poem is of permanent value depends, says Valéry, on its 'forme', not on its 'fond': 'L'expérience montre que les œuvres ne résistent à cette épreuve si redoutable, à cette concurrence pressée et toujours renouvelée que leur font les créations ultérieures que par une seule de leurs qualités, qui est la forme.'[2] However, as we have seen, the 'forme' of poetry

---

[1] *La Poétique de Valéry* (Paris, 1953), pp. 90-1
[2] Quoted from Hytier, op. cit., p. 81

is in fact an integral part of the 'fond', since the impression the poem conveys is created not only by what is said, but equally by how it is said. Analysis of the way poetry falls on the ear can therefore be relevant and valuable, although here too there are limitations, since the musical effect of poetry is a complex and composite one, taking place instantaneously, and a study dealing with one feature after another, unavoidable though such a procedure may be, is artificial. The most the critic can ever hope to achieve is to enrich his readers' appreciation of the stylistic potentialities of the verse.

CHAPTER III

Rhythm and Sounds

THE compromise between old and new habits which the reading of medieval verse entails is well illustrated by the poetry of Villon. Although few modern readers would take the trouble of observing those medieval intonations, pronunciations, and so on, about which something is known, it is necessary to pay some attention to them if the basic patterns and rhythms of the poetry are to be understood. Of the several treatises describing the structure of medieval verse, the most complete is that by Georges Lote: *Histoire du vers français.* This important work analyses medieval versification in some detail, and although not altogether free from certain prejudices and controversial matters, as will be seen presently, it provides an overall picture as complete and reliable as any.[1] Numerous quotations from fifteenth-century verse and from the fifteenth-century *Arts de seconde rhétorique* make it quite clear that Lote's references to the Middle Ages include the time of Villon quite as much as that of Chrétien de Troyes, and he himself specifies that the medieval verse structure he describes existed right up to the time of Malherbe.[2] This work is referred to extensively in the following pages.

Only two types of verse were used by Villon, both traditional: decasyllabic, limited to a few of his *ballades*, and

[1] Vol. I (Paris, 1949) vol. II (Paris, 1951) vol. III (Paris, 1955)
[2] Vol. I, p. 235

octosyllabic, used throughout the *Lais* and *Testament*, in several *ballades* and in the *rondeaux*. Most decasyllabic verse, since the time of the early hagiographic works some four centuries before that of the *Testament*, carried a caesura which usually affected the fourth syllable. According to Lote, this caesura was more of an accent than a pause. In the declaiming, or singing of decasyllabics—it should always be remembered that medieval verse was not designed to be read in silence—the fourth syllable was always accented, but whether or not a pause followed this accent depended on the meaning of the line.[1] Rhyme, on the other hand, involved both accent and pause, the difference between the two accents being that that of the caesura was a rising one, that of the rhyme falling. No other accents and no other pauses were allowed apart from these two. The drawback from which the decasyllabic suffered was that, despite the fact that it could be varied with a feminine *e* at the end of either hemistich (4 + *e*, 6 + *e*) or even at the caesura in lyric verse (3 + *e*), it was a rigid and stereotyped measure, for poets were not free to change the place of the caesura or to suppress it occasionally: '. . . la césure, dans toute forme césurée, est immuable et obligatoire'.[2] The same pattern had to be adhered to rigorously throughout. This explains in part Villon's preference for the octosyllabic, which on account of its shortness bore no caesura. Supple, light, permitting all kinds of rhythmic variation, it was admirably suited to him. None the less, he handled the decasyllabic with great competence. Less skilful poets found its rigidity a stumbling-block and were not always able to avoid having the caesura fall in the middle of a word, producing quaint effects as in this line of Froissart's:

[1] op. cit., vol. I, pp. 169, 173
[2] op. cit., vol. II, p. 240. Pp. 213-90 deals with the nature of the medieval caesura.

Comme le pá pillon a la chandelle[1]

Such awkward divisions were avoided by the better writers, and there is not a single instance amongst Villon's decasyllabic verse. It is true that he reduces the caesura at times to a pure metrical convention and on such occasions it harmonises little or not at all with the meaning:

Le temps qui ést passé ça en arriere . . . (*PD* XII, 14)

but there is not a single instance in his poetry of its falling in the middle of a word. Thus he did not write:

Amour plus dúre que fer a maschier . . .

but:

Amour duré plus que fer a maschier . . . (*T* 944)

Neither did he write:

Mains vaillans hómmes par moy mors et roidis . . . (*PD* XII, 9)

but, with his eye on the caesura and on the number of syllables, he made use of the alternative form *homs* existing in his day. Villon varies the strength of the caesura as was his right, but never allows it to make nonsense of a line in this age when metre and sense often collided: 'La métrique du Moyen Âge jette au sens les défis les plus incroyables.'[2] On the contrary he usually manages to arrange sense groups in such a way that they fit in with the metrical accents, which are made to fall on key words, so bringing out the full meaning:

Je meurs de séuf auprès de la fontáine,

Chault comme féu, et tremble dent a dént,

---

1 Quoted from Lote, op. cit., vol. I, p. 184
2 Lote, op. cit., vol. I, p. 244

En mon païs suis en terre loingtaine;
Lez ung brasier frissonne tout ardent;
Nu comme ung ver, vestu en president,
Je ris en pleurs et attens sans espoir;
Confort reprens en triste desespoir;
Je m'esjouÿs et n'ay plaisir aucun;
Puissant je suis sans force et sans povoir
Bien recueully, debouté de chascun.   (*PD* VII, I-IO)

The refrains of his decasyllabic *ballades* are usually models of their kind:

that of the prayer to the Virgin Mary:

En ceste foy je vueil vivre et mourir.

that of the *Épitaphe Villon*:

Mais priez Dieu que tous nous vueille absouldre!

that of the *Requeste au Parlement*:

Mere des bons et seur des benois anges!

that of the *Débat du Cuer et du Corps*:

Plus ne t'en dis.—Et je m'en passeray.

that of the *Contrediz de Franc Gontier*:

Il n'est tresor que de vivre a son aise.

that of the *Ballade de la Grosse Margot*:

En ce bordeau ou tenons nostre estat.

The caesura accent in Villon's verse falls on a non-final syllable only when a feminine *e* is silent because of a preceding or following juxtaposed vowel:

> . . . Et boivent eáu(e) tout au long de l'anée.
>
> Tous les oyseáulx d'icy en Babiloíne
>
> A tel escóll(e) une seule journée
>
> Ne me tendrói(ent), non une matinée.   (*T* 1494-7)

> Je leur tens eáu(e), frommage, pain et fruít.   (*T* 1597)

> Se je peussé vendre de ma santé
>
> A ung Lombárt, usurier par natúre,
>
> Faulte d'argént m'a si fort enchanté
>
> Que j'en prendrói(e), ce cuide, l'adventúre.   (*PD* x, 21-4)

> Et Proserpín(e) aux infernaulx palús   (*PD* v, 8)
>
> C'est qu'on luy cóul(e) au ventre son tresór   (*PD* v, 24)
>
> Ou gist il n'éntr(e) escler ne tourbillón.   (*PD* ix, 18)

On the other hand, the 'lyric caesura' is common in his poetry and accounts for 9·28 per cent of all his decasyllabics:

> Dame du ciél, regente terriénne,
>
> Emperieré des infernaux palús,
>
> Recevez móy, vostre humble chrestiénne,
>
> Que comprinsé soye entre vos esleús. . . .   (*T* 873-6)

51

Je m'en rissé, se tant peusse maschíer   (*T* 960)

De voz fillés si vous feist approuchíer   (*T* 1241)

De bien boiré ne fut oncques fetárt   (*T* 1251)

Occasionally a strong sense division occurs at a place other than the caesura, or alternatively the line may have no sense division whatever. The following table gives some idea of these differences:

Traditional 4-6 division in meaning as well as in metre	90·52%
6-4 sense division	4·45%
5-5 sense division	1·93%
7-3 sense division	1·16%
No sense division	1·93%

It is difficult to avoid all arbitrariness in these figures, since the 4-6 divisions vary a good deal in strength. Some have the force of a full stop, many of a comma, others are quite clear although they correspond to no punctuation mark, whilst a few are very weak; these last constitute, according to our calculations, 3·67 per cent of the total, and the figure of 90·52 per cent could be reduced by that amount. The fact remains that the majority of Villon's decasyllabics are carefully constructed according to the traditional pattern. It would be quite wrong to think of him as the vagabond poet, dashing off his verse in careless fashion, without a thought for the finer points of versification. Of course he takes liberties, like most poets of all ages, and the occasional line invites the reader to introduce some variety into the rhythm, particularly, be it noted, at or near the climax of a poem, dramatic or comical as the case may be. At such places the caesura may be reduced to a minimum, so giving a more rapid flow to the line:

La pluye nous a debuez et lavez . . .[1]   (*PD* xiv, 21)

---

[1] *pluye* counts as one syllable only in this line (cf. Burger, op. cit., p. 90), *debuez* as three.

Se feusses ung povre idiot et folet . . . (PD xi, 22)

(Se franc Gontier et sa compaigne Helaine)

Eussent ceste doulce vie hantee . . . (T 1483-4)

Se je peusse vendre de ma santé

A ung Lombart . . . (PD x, 21-2)

(Nobles seigneurs, ne souffrez empeschier)

L'ame du bon feu maistre Jehan Cotart. (T 1252-3)

This last line is the refrain of the *ballade* celebrating the drinking prowess of the late Jehan Cotart, and the caesura accent on *bon* enhances the humorous and ironical tone of the poem.

The 5-5 or 6-4 sense divisions, of which there is usually at least one, and not more than four, in each *ballade*, have the effect of making the line stand out from its context because a change of rhythm is involved, and this would inevitably occur even in the strictest declamation, where, as in the above examples, accent and pause at the caesura would be reduced to accent only. In a modern reading, if the editor's punctuation is respected, the contrast becomes even more startling. Lote protests that modern editions give a false idea of medieval verse whenever they punctuate according to sense divisions which fall outside the strict metrical pattern,[1] but it is surely not being unfaithful to the original to establish the fullest possible harmony between sense and rhythm. If there is any betrayal, it is the medieval declamation that suffers rather than the poetry itself. An example is provided by the refrain of the epistle addressed by Villon to his friends (PD ix), begging them to secure his release from prison:

Le lesserez la le povre Villon?

[1] op. cit., vol. I, p. 246

The *la* inevitably stands out, making one feel the full indignation of the poet: surely you are not intending to leave me in *that* place? The line becomes even more effective if read purely according to sense:

> Le lesserez lá, || le povre Villón?

The envoi of the Grosse Margot *ballade* illustrates this same feature. The line

> Nous deffuyóns onneur il nous deffúit . . .   (*T* 1626)

emphasises the degradation of the poet, his sense of shame and sin, all the more as it occurs after a series of lines every one of which has a very strongly marked 4-6 division. Here too a change of rhythm was already involved in medieval times, the caesura suddenly being limited to accent only, instead of accent and pause as the sense of the preceding lines requires, but in a modern reading this also can be brought out more forcefully:

> Je suis paillárt—la paillarde me súit.
>
> Lequel vault míeulx?—Chascun bien s'entresúit.
>
> L'ung vault l'autré;—c'est a mau rat mau chát.
>
> Ordure amóns,—ordure nous assúit;
>
> Nous deffuyóns *onneur*—il nous deffúit
>
> En ce bordéau ou tenons nostre estát.   (*T* 1622-7)

A similar example occurs in the *Débat*, when the Heart remonstrates with the Body:

> Ou la teste ás plus dure qu'ung jalét,
>
> Ou mieulx te plaíst qu'*onneur* ceste meschance! (*PD* xi, 25-6)

The *Louenge a la Court* is unusual in that it has two successive lines with this same construction:

Souvraine Cóurt, par qui sommes icý,
(ˊ)
Vous nous avez *gardé* de desconfíre.
(ˊ)
Or la langue *seule* ne peut souffíre

A vous rendre souffisantes louénges.　　(*PD* xv, 5-8)

More frequently, the caesura accent adds something to the meaning of the line, as in the refrains of the majority of Villon's *ballades*. A particularly striking example of this use of the metrical accent occurs in the envoi of the *Débat*:

Veulx tu vivré?—Dieu m'en doint la puissánce!—

Il te fault...—Quóy?—Remors de consciénce...(*PD* xi, 41-2)

In the first line *vivre* (with lyric caesura) and *puissance* are thrown into relief, but it is the second line that is of particular interest. The accent of the caesura falls on *Quoy*, and if we read the hemistich as it should be read, without an internal pause, this sudden interruption by the Body, which, as we have seen in an earlier chapter, marks the decisive turning-point in the poem, has the effect of a crack of a whip, quite sensational when viewed, as it must be, in the context of the whole poem. The full meaning here and elsewhere is not in what is said alone, but also in how it is said, how it is fitted into the verse pattern. The secret for the modern reader lies in rendering the poetry above all according to its basic meaning, but we must bear constantly in mind the nature of the framework which the verse was designed to fit.

*

In all French verse, modern as well as medieval, a slight pause should follow the rhyme.[1] A consequence is that, when meaning is left incomplete at the end of a line, the listener is

[1] See M. Grammont, *Le Vers français* (Paris, 4th ed., 1937), p. 35

held in suspense until the following line supplies the missing words. The second stanza of Villon's *Épitaphe* provides several instances:

> Se freres vous clamons, pas n'en devez
> *Avoir desdaing*, quoy que fusmes occis
> *Par justice*. Toutesfois, vous sçavez
> *Que tous hommes n'ont pas bon sens rassis.*   (*PD* xiv, 11-14)

Throughout the poem the only instances of overflow occur here. The poet is trying to make out some sort of case for himself and his fellow criminals. The essential features of his argument, the very points on which he might be expected to lay emphasis, appear as overflow: do not despise us, he is saying, we were slain by justice, it is true, but all men are not born wise. The other stanzas conform strictly to the usual decasyllabic pattern with sense divisions at the caesuras and ends of lines. Despite their emotional appeal they are more stiff and formal, rhetorical almost, whereas in the lines quoted, the conventional pattern is abruptly altered. The poet is no longer addressing a prayer, lyrical, but respectful and remote, to his fellow men. He appeals directly to them, in this simpler, more informal argument which comes out, not in a smooth mellifluous flow, but jerkily and unevenly, as ordinary speech itself. Paradoxically enough, this effect is heightened rather than lessened by the outer framework of the verse, even with caesura and rhyme fully respected. The lack of co-ordination between sense and metre, far from being the glaring fault that we are told it is in so much medieval verse, here adds enormously to the value of the poem, and is used to great artistic effect. As criticism stands today, Racine is praised for lines such as these:

> Mais tout n'est pas détruit, et vous en laissez vivre
> *Un* . . . Votre fils, seigneur, me défend de poursuivre . . .[1]

[1] See M. Grammont, op. cit., p. 36

whereas a medieval poet, achieving similar effects, is allowed no credit for them; in medieval verse, we are told, such features can be only a matter of chance, since aesthetic considerations must have been beyond these early writers.[1] Only in very recent years has this uncompromising attitude, the result of a long-standing prejudice, begun to change.

Villon's artistry with the decasyllabic line is also shown in the less solemn poems, as in the *ballade* concerning Jehan Cotart. It too contains a striking use of overflow in these lines summing up Cotart's drinking achievements:

> Brief, on n'eust sceu en ce monde serchier
> *Meilleur pyon*, pour boire tost et tart.
> Faictes entrer quant vous orrez huchier
> *L'ame du bon feu maistre Jehan Cotart.* (*T* 1258-61)

Meilleur pyon—'a better tippler'—is thrown into relief, emphasising that Cotart is king of them all. Also remarkable is the end of this stanza and all the others with the refrain presented each time as an overflow, whose effect is enhanced by the fact that it contains no sense division and is made of crisp-sounding words of one or two syllables; as we have seen above, the metrical accent also has a part to play in the impression created by this refrain, since it falls with gently ironical effect on *bon*. Each stanza has a merry ring about it, and ends in a burst of laughter.

Further examples are provided by the *Ballade de la Grosse Margot.* Villon is arguing with the whore on whose earnings he depends for a living, according, at any rate, to this particular

---

[1] For example, on the aesthetic use of masculine and feminine rhymes, Lote writes: 'Ce sont là, dans notre poésie française, des raffinements tout modernes qui supposent un sentiment artistique très développé et qui dépassent de beaucoup les conceptions médiévales' (op. cit., vol. II, p. 112). For further criticisms of the attitude of Lote and others, see P. Guiraud, *Les Sources médiévales de la poésie formelle: la rime* (Groningen, 1952), p. 4.

poem.[1] When she comes to bed empty-handed, Villon declares that her dress and petticoat will do to raise some money, whereat Margot waxes highly indignant:

> Par les costés se prent, 'c'est Antecrist'
> *Crie*, et jure par la mort Jhesucrist
> *Que non fera.* Lors j'empoingne ung esclat ... (*T* 1606-8)

The angry screams and wild gesticulations of the harlot are well portrayed in the verse, the verb *crie* echoing the harsh *cr* sounds of *Antecrist* and being flung in suddenly as an overflow, as also is Margot's indignant rejection of her lover's suggestion. The modern reader is free to bring out the full force of the second line by observing the sense pause after *Crie*.

★

As regards octosyllabic verse, only the earliest texts had a caesura. By the twelfth century caesuras in this type of verse had become rare, doubtless because of the difficulty of maintaining a metrical accent in so short a line, and also because of the jangling monotony of the 4-4 pattern. The early writers of romance made free use of overflow, and Villon is following in their footsteps when he exploits every type of octosyllabic line imaginable. The medieval attitude towards this line seems to have been a good deal more tolerant than towards the decasyllabic. Here, too, variety is not merely an end in itself for Villon, nor is it simply due to the strain of having to assemble a small number of syllables in one line. It is often used artistically, revealing, if not originality, at least his complete mastery of form. For example, in his lines on poverty, consoling himself with the idea that it is better to be

---

[1] Opinions are divided as to whether or not Margot was an actual person, but most critics agree that this poem does reflect some aspects of Villon's life, even if only indirectly.

poor and alive than to have been rich and to be dead, he writes:

> Mieulx vault vivre soubz gros bureau
> *Povre*, qu'avoir esté seigneur
> Et pourrir soubz riche tombeau. (*T* 286-8)

The whole trend of the argument and the spirit of the passage demand that the word *povre* should bear emphasis, and indeed the construction of these lines throws the word—a *leit-motiv* in itself—into relief, since it forms an overflow and is isolated from the rest of its line by a sense division. The same construction occurs in the *Lais*, where Villon is lamenting over the cruelty of his mistress, on account of whom, so he says, he must leave the capital:

> Combien que le depart me soit
> *Dur*, si faut il que je l'eslongne . . . (*L* 49-50)

The very construction is part of the meaning, showing what a bitter blow it was for him to have to take his leave. How harshly she has treated him!

> Veult et ordonne que j'endure
> *La mort*, et que plus je ne dure. (*L* 36-7)

Finally he resigns himself to the fact that she will not grant him her 'grace', and leave he must:

> Puis qu'el ne me veult impartir
> *Sa grace*, il me convient partir. (*L* 44-5)

The same device is used in lighter vein. Making a legacy to Maistre Robert Valee in the *Lais*, Villon writes:

> J'ordonne principalement
> Qu'on luy baille legierement . . . (*L* 100-1)

'My main request is that he be given without delay . . .' What is this legacy to be? The answer comes with swift mockery at the beginning of the next line: 'Mes brayes . . .' 'My breeches'. In fact constructions of this sort abound in Villon's poetry, appearing in practically every stanza. Admittedly there are some which serve no purpose other than mere convenience:

> Ou temps qu'Alixandre regna,
> Ung homs nommé Diomedes
> Devant luy on luy amena,
> Engrillonné poulces et des
> Comme ung larron, car il fut *des*
> *Escumeurs* que voions courir . . .   (*T* 129-34)

but many serve to bring out some particular point.

In some cases the initial word of a line is isolated from the rest even though it does not constitute an overflow:

> Mais que ce jeune bacheler
> Laissast ces jeunes bacheletes?
> *Non*! et le deust on vif brusler
> Comme ung chevaucheur d'escouvetes.   (*T* 665-8)

The *non* explodes at the beginning of the line, driving home Villon's argument that the young man cannot resist pursuing the young maidens, however foolish he makes himself. This is a trick of style common to many of Villon's predecessors though none surpassed him in the skill with which he used it. An isolated monosyllable in the interior of a line stands out in much the same way:

> Ha! vieillesse felonne et fiere,
> Pourquoi m'as si tost abatue?
> Qui me tient, *qui*, que ne me fiere,[1]
> Et qu'a ce coup je ne me tue?   (*T* 457-60)

The withered beauty is cursing old age, which has destroyed the good looks she once possessed, and has brought her

[1] *Qui* here has the meaning 'What . . .?' rather than 'Who . . .?'

loneliness and destitution, since no man has any interest in her now. The repetition of *qui* at so short an interval and its isolated position between the two clauses have the effect of laying great stress on the word. The very construction reveals the sorrow and despair of the old woman.

In the *Ballade des Dames du Temps Jadis* Villon laments over the passing away of the most famous ladies the world has known:

> Ou sont ilz, *ou*, Vierge souvraine,
> Mais ou sont les neiges d'antan? (*T* 351-2)

The repetition of *ou* underlines the pathos of the question, and this is in fact the climax of the whole poem.

Besides serving for emphasis, Villon's sense divisions vary the pace of his octosyllabics, sometimes to particular effect. Thus, in the following passage concerning the bishop of Orléans on whose orders he had been imprisoned at Meung-sur-Loire, the first three lines have the same 4-4 division—a question solely of rhythm, not caesura—and the last line, which abruptly breaks this pattern, stands out from the rest on account of the change in rhythm:

> Mon seigneur n'est—ne mon evesque,
> Soubz luy ne tiens—s'il n'est en friche;
> Foy ne luy doy—n'hommage avecque,
> Je ne suis son *serf*—ne sa biche . . . (*T* 9-12)

The hiss of the sibilants in the last line adds to its effect. The line is spat out suddenly and viciously, leaving no doubt about Villon's hatred for this person. One may compare for construction the *Ballade des Femmes de Paris*. A series of lines with long-sounding, awkward names, each line divided into two or more segments by sense divisions, imparts a slow, limping gait to the verse, but a smooth, racy, monosyllabic refrain follows, suggesting the ease and quickness with which the women of Paris get the better of others:

> Mais, soient Lombardes, Rommaines,
> Genevoises, a mes perilz,
> Pimontoises, Savoisiennes,
> Il n'est bon bec que de Paris.   (*T* 1519-22)

Variety is exploited for stress or pace, throwing emphasis on a key word in a passage, or suggesting rapidity or slowness at the wish of the poet. One has only to compare the refrain of the *Ballade des Dames du Temps Jadis* with that of the *Double Ballade* on the vanity of love, to realise what a supple and versatile line the octosyllabic could be in the hands of a poet like Villon. How much longer the slow-moving, sad-echoing refrain of the former sounds: 'Mais ou sont les neiges d'antan?' compared with the mocking refrain of the latter, with its insistence that the happy man is the one who has nothing to do with love: 'Bien est eureux qui riens n'y a!' How easily this trips off the tongue! It is a superbly rhythmical line, mounting smoothly to a climax with *eureux*, the second half of the line descending with equal smoothness. The wittiness of the remark is enhanced by the very structure. The same refrain is used by another fifteenth-century poet, Guillaume Alexis, with a slight but significant variation: 'Bien eureux est qui riens n'y a!' Villon's is the original.[1] That of Guillaume Alexis is dominated by the desire to juxtapose adverb and adjective, a grammatical consideration admirably suited to prose; with Villon sound and rhythm take precedence over syntax.

★

Just as the structure of verse can contribute directly to its meaning, so too can the sound patterns. Although this

[1] cf. Guillaume Alexis, *Œuvres poétiques*, S.A.T.F., vol. I, p. 121

'imitative harmony' or 'sound symbolism'—ironically enough the subject seems doomed to have a clumsy-sounding title— has for long been studied, it is only in comparatively recent times that it has been given a thorough treatment in works on versification, stylistics and semantics. A good deal of scorn has been poured on it by some writers. Are we, they ask, to imagine a poet, wishing to evoke some particular feeling, resorting to a table of sounds as a mathematician resorts to logarithms? Does the poet say to himself: now this must sound sad, so I must use . . . let me see . . . ah, yes! nasal vowels and sibilant consonants? The answer, surely, is that scholars and critics need their sound tables in their endeavours to understand and explain poetry, but not so the poet. What the critics analyse so painstakingly comes intuitively to the poet, endowed with keener hearing and sensitivity than most people. It is an integral part of his art as a musician whose notes are made up of vowels and consonants.

The sceptic may greet with scorn any attempt to find such harmonies in pre-Renaissance poetry, and as mentioned earlier in connection with rhythm, it has been categorically stated that subtleties of this nature were quite beyond the early French poets. What is overlooked is that in Villon's time poetry had not long been dissociated from music and the two arts retained connections far closer than any they possess nowadays. 'Rhétorique et Musique sont une mesme chose' wrote Jean Lemaire de Belges,[1] an idea also put forward by Jean Molinet and earlier by Eustache Deschamps. It has been pointed out that refrains such as *Mirontaine* aim at pleasing the ear,[2] and it is worth while adding that most of these are in fact medieval inventions, and that numbers existed in the Middle

---

[1] Quoted by J. Frappier in his edition of *La Concorde des deux langages* (Paris, 1947), p. xl.
[2] J. Marouzeau, *Précis de stylistique française* (Paris, 3rd ed., 1950), p. 18

Ages which do so no longer: *Vadeurelidele*, *Vadeurelidot*, etc. Furthermore, it has been said of the Provençal lyric, whose influence on the poetry of the north was profound, that 'the harmony of the words is of greater significance than their logical content'.[1] Then, as now, poets were preoccupied with manner of expression as much as with whatever they wished to express. Such is the very essence of poetry, and it was not the seventeenth century which saw the birth of this conception in France, but the eleventh century, and earlier still if the medieval Latin lyric be included.

For an increasing number of critics nowadays, medieval poets are far from being the primitives they have sometimes been made out to be. It has for long been acknowledged that they were familiar with such relatively simple devices as alliteration, but more intricate sound effects are now being sought in even the earliest works. It has been claimed, for example, that the famous death scene of Roland was made by the poet to assonate in *-i* because this high-pitched sound was able to contribute to the mingled grief and triumph of these lines:

> Li quens Rollant se jut desuz un pin,
> Envers Espaigne en ad turnét sun vis;
> De plusurs choses a remembrer li prist:
> De tantes teres cum li bers conquist,
> De dulce France, des humes de sun lign,
> De Carlemagne, sun seignor ki·l nurrit;
> Ne poet müer n'en plurt e ne suspirt . . .[2]

Similar effects have been seen recently in the lyric poetry of the Middle Ages, although Villon has received comparatively little attention from this point of view. None the less, harmony between sound and sense is a feature of his verse. The sound

[1] W. D. Elcock, *The Romance Languages* (London, 1960), p. 383
[2] See P. Le Gentil, *La Chanson de Roland* (Paris, 1955), p. 177

patterns of his gayer and more farcical pieces are not at all the same as those of his lines of reminiscence and melancholy. Differences in this sphere reflect those differences in rhythm analysed above.

Villon's protagonist, the aged harlot, is giving advice to the younger members of her profession:

> Or y pensez, belle Gaultiere[1]
> Qui escoliere souliez estre,[2]
> Et vous, Blanche la Savetiere,
> Or est il temps de vous congnoistre.
> Prenez a destre et a senestre;
> N'espargnez homme, je vous prie:
> Car vielles n'ont ne cours ne estre,
> Ne que monnoye qu'on descrie.
>
> Et vous, la gente Saulciciere
> Qui de dancier estes adestre,
> Guillemete la Tapiciere,
> Ne mesprenez vers vostre maistre:
> Tost vous fauldra clorre fenestre;
> Quant deviendrez vielle, flestrie,
> Plus ne servirez qu'ung viel prestre,
> Ne que monnoye qu'on descrie . . .   (T 533-48)

These are some of the most delightful of Villon's lines, achieving a remarkable harmony between sound and sense. The sharp-sounding palatal vowels *e*, *i* and *ie* recur constantly and stand out all the more as they provide the rhyme patterns. Throughout the entire *ballade* the rhymes are all feminine, and it is almost impossible to avoid drawling the *-iere* suffix which strengthens the note of mockery. The whole *ballade* has a

---

[1] *Gaultiere*, the reading of the four principal sources, is defined as follows by Cotgrave: 'A whore, punke, drab, queane, gill, flirt, strumpet, cockatrice, mad wench, common hackney, good one.'

[2] For the reading *escoliere* in preference to *m'escoliere* see F. Lecoy, op. cit., p. 511.

jocular ring about it. The lilt of 'Qui de dancier estes adestre' suggests the swift movement, the swirl and clatter of the dancing girl, maintained in the following lines with 'vos*tre* mais*tre*' and 'c*lorre* fenes*tre*'. To feel the effect of this verse it is essential that it should be read aloud. It goes rollicking gaily along, a wonderful example of the *gaulois* side of Villon, a cynical treatment of the *carpe diem* theme all the more impressive when read in its context in the *Testament*, for it has grown out of and supplanted a mood of sorrow and bitterness at the passing of youth and the ravages wrought on the body by age. Even a reader with no understanding of these lines could hardly suppose them to be concerned with melancholy. The *Double Ballade*, with its jeering remarks on love, follows after a brief interlude, and it too reads quickly and gaily, with rhymes in *-ez*, *-estes* and *-y a*:

> Pour ce, amez tant que vouldrez,
> Suyvez assemblees et festes,
> En la fin ja mieulx n'en vauldrez
> Et n'y romperez que vos testes;
> Folles amours font les gens bestes:
> Salmon en ydolatria,
> Samson en perdit ses lunetes.
> Bien est eureux qui riens n'y a!   (*T* 625-32)

The refrain, as pointed out earlier, trips smoothly off the tongue, and with its sharp *-y a* rhyme seems to end each stanza in a derisive shout, a scornful 'yah!' at those who take love seriously. Much the same irreverent mood is reflected in the *Ballade et Oroison* written to celebrate Jehan Cotart's prowess at drinking, and which we have had occasion to mention earlier for its rhythm. The second stanza is worth quoting in full:

> Jadis extraict il fut de vostre ligne,
> Luy qui buvoit du meilleur et plus chier,

> Et ne deust il avoir vaillant ung pigne;
> Certes, sur tous, c'estoit ung bon archier;
> On ne luy sceut pot des mains arrachier;
> De bien boire ne fut oncques fetart.
> Nobles seigneurs, ne souffrez empeschier
> L'ame du bon feu maistre Jehan Cotart!   (T 1246-53)

All is swift and staccato with rhymes in *-igne* and *-ier* and the predilection shown for crisp words of one or two syllables, particularly in the refrain. Here too Villon is in sprightly mood, and both rhythm and sounds make this quite clear. Sometimes alliteration is used along with rhythm to achieve a similar effect:

> A folz, folles, a sotz et sotes,
> Qui s'en vont siflant six a six,
> A vecyes et mariotes,[1]
> Je crie a toutes gens mercis.   (T 1980-3)

The *Ballade de la Grosse Margot* also deserves mention:

> Puis paix se fait, et me fait ung gros pet,
> Plus enflee qu'ung vlimeux escharbot.
> Riant, m'assiet son poing sur mon sommet,
> Gogo me dit, et me fiert le jambot . . .[2]   (T 1611-14)

The sharp *e* and *o* sounds of the masculine rhymes, repeated several times in the interior of the lines, the alliterative use of plosive and fricative consonants (*p*, *f* and *s* in particular), the preference shown once more for short words of only one or two syllables, all evoke the crude sounds of the place Villon is describing. Sense, sounds and rhythm harmonise, and the meaning resides in all three.

If we turn now to the passages of melancholy which occur

---

[1] For the reading of this line, see F. Lecoy, op. cit., pp. 507-8.
[2] The meaning given by Thuasne for *jambot* is incorrect; cf. F. Lecoy, op. cit., p. 505.

in the early part of the *Testament*, we find a radical difference
in sounds:

> Ou sont les gracieux gallans
> Que je suivoye ou temps jadis,
> Si bien chantans, si bien parlans,
> Si plaisans en faiz et en dis? (*T* 225-8)

The nostalgia of these lines makes them ring solemnly in the
ears and demands that they should be read slowly. In fact it
is quite impossible to read them with the rapid gait of the
Double Ballade or that of the advice given by the Belle Heaulmière. These octosyllabic lines are considerably longer and
more weighty to the ear than the decasyllabic lines of the
Cotart and Margot *ballades*. Their wistful effect is owed in
considerable measure to the sounds themselves. Nasal vowels,
of which there is such an accumulation here, are conducive to
an atmosphere of languor and sadness. A third of the vowels
in these lines are nasals, and they occupy a prominent position
since they provide one of the rhymes, echoed in the interior of
two of the lines by *chantans* and *plaisans*. The dominant consonant is *s*, always a versatile sound in poetry, harmonising
with sense to produce a variety of impressions and moods:
'C'est l'angoisse causée par la peur ou la tristesse, le frisson
produit par le froid moral comme par le froid physique.'[1] Its
role here is very different from that which it has in the Grosse
Margot *ballade*. Balanced this time with nasal vowels and
given prominence in the rhymes *dis* and *jadis*, where the voice
dwells on the sound at the pause, it is in an altogether different
key, and its soft sibilance helps to convey the poet's melancholy.
The overall effect is produced by the whole pattern of inter-
woven sounds, depending on the choice and arrangement of
words. The result here is the low pitch and slow, heavy-footed
movement of:

[1] M. Grammont, op. cit., p. 304

Si bien chantans, si bien parlans,
Si plaisans en faiz et en dis.   (*T* 227-8)

The *Regrets de la Belle Heaulmière* bring the melancholy
section of the *Testament* to a climax with the picture of the
pathetic old women squatting around their tiny fire:

Ainsi le bon temps regretons
Entre nous, povres vielles sotes
Assises bas, a crouppetons,
Tout en ung tas comme pelotes,
A petit feu de chenevotes
Tost allumees, tost estaintes;
Et jadis fusmes si mignotes! . . .
Ainsi en prent a mains et maintes.   (*T* LVI)

Here too almost a third of the vowels are nasals, and they again
provide one of the rhymes. Prominent amongst the remainder
is the *e* of the article *le* and feminine endings. This so-called
'mute *e*', muted rather than mute in French verse, involves
little effort of articulation and in consequence falls very softly
on the ear, producing an effect not unlike that of a rest in
music.

No survey of the sound patterns of Villon's verse could be
complete without mention of his most celebrated poem, the
Ballade des Dames du Temps Jadis, whose aesthetic qualities have
been made the object of a special study by Leo Spitzer:

Dictes moy ou, n'en quel pays,
Est Flora la belle Rommaine,
Archipiades, ne Thaïs,
Qui fut sa cousine germaine,
Echo parlant quant bruyt on maine
Dessus riviere ou sus estan,
Qui beaulté ot trop plus qu'humaine.
Mais ou sont les neiges d'antan?   (*T* 329-36)

Nasal vowels and sibilant consonants are once more prominent in the rhymes: *pays (pa-is)*: *Thaïs*; *Rommaine*: *germaine*: *Maine*: *humaine* (still nasal in Villon's day, with the sound *-ẽne*); and *estan*: *antan*. The ends of the lines have strongly marked sense divisions, and as a result the rhyme sounds are given their fullest possible value. The reader cannot avoid lingering over them, and they assume a haunting effect, culminating in the well-known refrain. The clear pauses at the ends of the lines and in the interior of some of them, and the spacing out of the more resonant sounds which are constantly recalled throughout the rhymes help to create the atmosphere of the poem.

Villon's art is revealed in the sound patterns of all his moods, sad or merry, serious or mocking. Examples abound in the *Testament*, whether he is depicting his hatred of his tormentor:

Je ne suis son serf ne sa biche . . .   (*T* 12)

the noise and gaiety of the street crowds:

Qui s'en vont siflant six a six . . .   (*T* 1981)

or the nostalgic yearning for beauty that has gone for ever:

Mais ou sont les neiges d'antan?   (*T* 336, 344, etc.)

*

Poetry of all languages and epochs depends for its success on a blending of numerous traits, each of which must be kept within its own limits. Villon was writing in an age when rhyme was allowed to run riot, becoming very often the sole *raison d'être* of the verse of the *Rhétoriqueurs*, for whom 'to rhyme' meant also 'to pun'. Here, for example, are some verses of Guillaume Crétin mourning the death of Guillaume de Bissipat:

O mort *helas*!
Tu as cherché avoir ce corps *et l(e) as.*
Mon triste cueur de vivre au monde *est las,*
Car lui et moy sommes liez *es las*
　　　D'aspres douleurs.[1]

Villon remained aloof from such fads. They are reflected, admittedly, in the mocking ditty:

　　　Jenin l'Avenu
　　　Va-t-en aux estuves;
　　　Et toy la venu,
　　　Jenin l'Avenu

　　　Si te lave nud
　　　Et te baigne es cuves.
　　　Jenin l'Avenu,
　　　Va-t-en aux estuves.　　　　　　　*(PD* vi)

Here at least, there is a quite acceptable harmony between the puns and the sense of the poem. It seems a pity to rob Villon of this ingenious cry of derision, yet the attribution of it to him is very likely wrong.[2] An occasional line reflects the conjuring with words so characteristic of the later fifteenth century:

　　　Quant de *sonner* est a *son erre*　　　　　　*(T* 1907)

and now and again he uses a 'rime équivoque' covering several syllables:

　　　. . . Joinctes et nerfs croistre et *estendre.*
　　　Corps femenin, qui tant *es tendre* . . .　　　　*(T* 324-5)

---

[1] ed. K. Chesney (Paris, 1932), p. 75
[2] See A. Jeanroy and E. Droz, *Deux MSS. de François Villon* (Paris, 1932), pp. XIV-XV.

Rhymes of this sort often seem accidental rather than deliberate in his poetry, and are never the main feature of the verse. The rhyme he favours is a moderately rich one which, in the case of the masculine, includes the consonant preceding the last tonic vowel of the line, e.g. *T* 665 *bacheler*: *brusler*. On the other hand, like other poets who normally chose a moderately rich rhyme, he made frequent use of feminine rhymes without this reinforcing consonant, e.g. *T* 690 *aultre*: *faultre*, since even the simplest feminine rhymes were dissyllabic, although the final *e* did not count in the measure of the line.[1] The rhymes of the following stanza typify those of the *Testament*:

> Icy n'y a ne ris ne *jeu*.
> Que leur valut avoir chev*ances*,
> N'en granz liz de parement *jeu*,
> Engloutir vins en grosses p*ances*,
> Mener joye, festes et d*ances*,
> Et de ce prest estre a toute h*eure*?
> Toutes faillent telles plais*ances*,
> Et la coulpe si en dem*eure*.   (*T* CLXI)

A complete analysis of the rhymes of the *Lais* and the *Testament* has yielded the following results:

	Masculine	
Assonantes		
(e.g. *T* 1721 *corps*: *mors*)	*Le Lais* 9·89%	*Le Testament*: 15·74%
Consonantes		
(*T* 1728 *Vings*: Pro*vins*)	41·76%	42·62%
Léonines simples		
(*T* 1761 *pourris*: *nourris*)	19·78%	29·18%
Léonines parfaites		
(*T* 1849 *difficulté*: *faculté*)	18·68%	8·52%
Léonines plus-que-parfaites		
(*L* 5 *conseiller*: *conseiller*)	9·89%	3·94%

[1] See Lote, op. cit., vol. II, pp. 145-6

Feminine

	Le Lais:	*Le Testament*:
Léonines simples		
(e.g. *T* 1739 p*ances*:d*ances*)	23·53%	46·28%
Léonines parfaites		
(*T* 1753 v*ies*: ser*vies*)	41·18%	35·68%
Léonines plus–que–parfaites		
(*T* 1771 in*ique*: Dom*inique*)	35·29%	18·04%

The differences between the two poems have been discussed in an earlier chapter.[1] They show that Villon's evolution in this sphere was the reverse of that of his century, for whereas long and intricate rhymes were to become more and more the fashion in the course of the century, Villon's became shorter and simpler in his later works, although there is a notable tendency in the *Testament* for the sounds of the rhymes to echo more closely the meaning of the verse. This applies, as the examples quoted earlier have shown, to the light-hearted passages as much as to the serious ones. Length achieved purely for its own sake gives way to something infinitely more subtle, more fundamentally satisfying to the ear, and altogether more important from the aesthetic point of view: harmony between sound and sense.

The attitude of a poet towards rhyme is revealed most clearly in the two extreme categories: the longest, covering three syllables or more, and the shortest, the masculine *rimes assonantes*, limited to the last vowel of the line and the consonants following it. It will be observed from the above tables that Villon by no means banishes the *rimes assonantes* from his verse, and resorts more frequently to them as time goes on. A study of these rhymes in the two testaments and in the miscellaneous *ballades* has given the following results:

1 Eighty-seven of Villon's assonating rhymes, that is slightly more than 65 per cent of the total of such rhymes, involve

[1] See above, pp. 23-6

monosyllables as one or both of the rhyming words. In fact it had long been traditional for poets who usually avoided the poorest rhymes, such as Jean de Meun, to accept them in the case of monosyllables.[1] The categories that follow were also traditionally allowed.

2 Sixteen involve rhymes in which the tonic vowel is preceded by another vowel (*cruel*, *perpetuel*, etc.) and of these sixteen, eleven also involve monosyllables or proper names: *mal*: *official* (*T* 745); *Riou*: *lou* (*T* 1126), etc.

3 Thirty-eight involve proper names; twenty-six of these belong to one or other of the above categories.

4 Thirty involve words in which the tonic vowel was *ie*; most of them are monosyllables: *rien*: *bien* (*T* 1303), etc.

5 Eight involve words ending in *-or*, *-our*, *-eur*; *amours*: *doulours* (*T* 622). Here too, a monosyllable or proper name was usually involved as well: *jours*: *amours* (*T* 1067).

6 Seven involve Latin words or learned forms; *reliqua*: *cetera* (*T* 742).

Only nine remain belonging to no category traditionally accepted—accepted it should be added, out of necessity, since for most of these words it was difficult to find a rich rhyme. Those unaccounted for, and which could be considered as poor rhymes from the medieval point of view, are the following:

advocat: *estat* (*T* 1022)   *esclat*: *estat* (*T* 1608)

The second example concerns the refrain of the *Ballade de la Grosse Margot*. Twice in this poem Villon manages to rhyme *estat* with monosyllables *plat* and *chat*, and once with the Latin expression *bene stat*.

---

[1] See *Le Roman de la Rose*, ed. E. Langlois, S.A.T.F., vol. I (1914), p. 56; and E. Freymond, 'Über den reichen Reim bei altfranzösischen Dichtern bis zum Anfang des XIV. Jahrh.' in *Zeitschrift für Romanische Philologie*, vol. VI (1882), pp. 1-36, 177-215; see in particular pp. 30-3.

commun: *chascun* (*PD* VII, 33)

This rhyme appears at the end of the *Ballade du Concours de Blois*; *chascun*, like *estat* in the Grosse Margot *ballade*, belongs to the refrain. Villon rhymes the word once with *aucun*, twice with monosyllables, and it is only when he has to find a fourth rhyme that he resorts to an unsatisfactory one.

bureau: *tombeau* (*T* 286)   *cuveaulx*: *drappeaulx*: *bordeaulx* (*T*1447)

These rhymes were probably a good deal more satisfying to the ear in Villon's day than they are nowadays, since the triphthong -*eau* had not been reduced completely to a single sound.[1] The remaining examples occur in series of three rhymes, one of which is assonating, the others rich; all appear in *ballades* where the strain of finding the same rhymes for each stanza has forced the poet to take some liberties, and two involve the -*eau* ending:

effort: confort: *ressort*	(*PD* I, 26)
sans espoir: desespoir: *povoir*	(*PD* VII, 6)
meseaulx: houseaulx: *blereaulx*	(*T* 1427)
morceaulx: *bluteaulx*: pourceaulx	(*T* 1452)

Such rhymes are not intrinsically bad, and are unsatisfactory only according to the conventions of the age. That Villon respected these conventions is shown by his keeping these dissyllabic assonating rhymes to a minimum. This is a rare instance of poets of later ages being less inhibited than their ancestors; Racine does not hesitate to rhyme *tombeau* with *fardeau*, La Fontaine *climats* with *trépas*, Hugo *soleil* with *vermeil*, Verlaine *perdu* with *battu*, etc.

More reprehensible in Villon's poetry are several instances of assonance or approximate rhyme, although not all are as bad as they may appear to the modern reader: *enfle*: *Temple*

---

[1] See M. K. Pope, *From Latin to Modern French* (Manchester, 1934; reprinted 1952), paras. 538-9.

(*T* 1027); *Bible: Evangille* (*T* 1507); *peuple: seule* (*PD* VIII, 17); *Grenobles: Doles* (*T* 401); *bransle: tremble* (*T* 1904).[1] In each of these cases, slurring of the consonant immediately preceding the *l* would give a satisfactory rhyme, and since associations of this nature were not uncommon in and long before Villon's day, it is likely that such pronunciations existed.[2] There are three other instances of assonance: *fuste: feusse* (*T* 142); *dame: d'asne* (*T* 1564); *prophetes: fesses* (*T* 806). The remaining cases involve the slurring of a final *s: issue: bossues* (*T* 517; cf. *T* 562, *T* 634) or final *e: Troyes: trois* (*T* 614, cf. *T* 1338).

It is clear that rhyme was not such an overriding factor with Villon that he was above accepting the occasional assonance—particularly, be it noted, in his later work, the *Testament*, where length and exactness were no longer the primary considerations in matters of rhyme—but the cases of assonance and of assonating rhyme form only a small proportion of the total, less than 10 per cent in fact. Throughout his poetry Villon aims above all at a rhyme sufficiently rich to please the ear without its drawing undue attention to itself. It plays its part well in his poetry, but is never the star turn. Rhyme in fact remained very much Villon's servant and never became his master as it did with Guillaume Crétin and others of his school.

*

Analyses of this sort, taking each feature in turn, cannot as pointed out in the preceding chapter, really do the poetry full justice. Its force and individuality depend on a subtle combination of many traits, chief amongst them being the

---

[1] See G. Paris, 'Villoniana' in *Romania*, 30 (1901), p. 369.
[2] See H. Chatelain, *Recherches sur le vers français au XVe siècle* (Paris, 1908), pp. 48-9; *Le Roman de Thèbes*, ed. L. Constans, S.A.T.F., vol. II, pp. lxvii-lxviii; and *Villon, Œuvres*, ed. L. Thuasne, 3 vols., (Paris, 1923), vol. I, pp. 113-14. For a different point of view see Lote, op. cit., vol. III, p. 324.

trinity: sense, sounds (particularly rhyme) and rhythm. To decide that one is more important than the others is arbitrary. For Boileau, in the seventeenth century, sense had to predominate, whereas for Valéry, in the twentieth, form (i.e. arrangement of sounds, rhythm, etc.) is paramount.[1] In the last resort, however, the impression the poem makes on the reader or listener is due to all these elements, not one rather than another. All three create the 'meaning' of lines such as these:

> Et meure Paris ou Helaine,
> Quiconques meurt, meurt a douleur
> Telle qu'il pert vent et alaine;
> Son fiel se creve sur son cuer,
> Puis sue, Dieu scet quelle sueur!
> Et n'est qui de ses maux l'alege:
> Car enfant n'a, frere ne seur,
> Qui lors voulsist estre son plege.   (*T* XL)

The deliberate, painful hammering on *meurt* finds an echo in the principal rhyme: doul*eur*: c*uer*; s*ueur*: s*eur*, and it is most significant that, in this stanza of the *Testament*, surely one of the most deeply felt that Villon ever wrote, the main rhyme is a very short one, but the choice of its vowel sound to suit the tenor of the passage is admirable. The sound of these grim, fear-haunted lines is harsh and unpleasant; it grates on the ear, and we are far from the soft harmonies of the *Ballade des Dames*. Their halting, uneven gait adds to the horror they express; 'meurt a douleur' stands out as a result of the chiasmus, and the following line, coming as an overflow, falls with emphasis on the ear. 'Puis sue' forms a sharp, staccato beginning to its line and echoes like a cry of terror in the ear of the reader. Like all Villon's themes, this one was common enough in French medieval poetry. What he is saying here is trite in the extreme. It is *how* he says it that counts.

[1] See above, p. 45

77

CHAPTER IV

Syntax and Vocabulary

IT IS impossible to read far into Villon's works without being struck by the concentrated, elliptical nature of his language. We have only to turn to the opening lines of his major work:

> En l'an de mon trentiesme aage,
> Que toutes mes hontes j'eus beues,
> Ne du tout fol, ne du tout sage,
> Non obstant maintes peines eues,
> Lesquelles j'ay toutes receues
> Soubz la main Thibault d'Aussigny . . .
> S'evesque il est, seignant les rues,
> Qu'il soit le mien je le regny.
>
> Mon seigneur n'est ne mon evesque,
> Soubz luy ne tiens, s'il n'est en friche . . .　　　(T 1-10)

It is at once made clear that Villon is writing about himself at the age of thirty, though his account in these opening lines reads more like a series of disconnected jottings than a properly arranged autobiography. We are at once taken into his confidence and find ourselves in the midst of his affairs, hearing of disgrace and suffering, but learning little or nothing of what it is really all about. An impression of near incoherence is created. He takes it for granted that his readers know who is writing—there is nothing corresponding to the 'Je, Françoys Villon, escollier' of the *Lais*—and he expects us to accept without question his remarks on the cruelty and injustice shown him by the bishop. Not a word on why he had been in prison. Here and elsewhere he gives his own obviously biased comments on episodes in his life without explaining just what had happened, a necessary reticence, no doubt, in view of his undeniably evil ways, which other sources, less discreet and less subjective, have revealed to us.

The language of this first stanza deserves closer attention:

En l'an de mon trentiesme aage . . .

The meaning is quite clear: 'In the thirtieth year of my life . . .' but the construction is puzzling: 'In the year of my thirtieth . . .?' Modern editors have explained that *aage* could mean 'year of one's life', but this does not solve the problem. The real difficulty is to know why Villon did not use the more common and logical construction: 'En l'an trentiesme de mon aage', the reading advocated by Gaston Paris[1] even though not a single manuscript of Villon's work contains it. It is true that similar expressions from contemporary texts usually associate the numeral with *an* rather than with *aage*: 'ou XXXVIe an de mon aage', 'en l'an XXXIXe de l'aage d'icellui translateur', 'au XXXVe an de mon aage', 'ou XVIe an de son aage', etc.[2] Only rarely does the numeral appear with *aage*, and then usually *an* is omitted altogether: 'en mon aage soixante et dixiesme'. The sole example resembling Villon's line which has been brought to light is the following, and the resemblance is only slight:

---

[1] 'Villoniana' in *Romania*, 30 (1901), pp. 361-2. The advantage of Paris's emendation is that it makes *aage* a word of two syllables as elsewhere in Villon's poetry (*T* 1276, *T* 1832, *PD* XI, 12) instead of three syllables, but, as Burger points out (op. cit., p. 13) Villon did not always avoid hiatus, and the final *e* of *trentiesme* may very well have been sounded, so that even with the word order as it stands in the MSS., *aage* could be dissyllabic, initial *a* having become silent.

[2] See Thuasne, op. cit., vol. II, pp. 76-80

La noble dame sur ce point trespassa,
De quoy ce fut ung merveilleux dommage,
Car jamais l'an en vie ne passa
Avec six moys le quatorziesme aage . . .

but this may be accounted for by the exigencies of metre and rhyme. The free choice open to Villon ('En l'an trentiesme . . .' or 'En l'an de mon trentiesme . . .') was not available to this writer in these circumstances, and the parallel between this couplet and the line of Villon, to which both Foulet and Thuasne point,[1] is misleading. The effect of Villon's order is to change the expression from a logical one: 'In the thirtieth year of my life', to a pleonastic one, 'In the year of my thirtieth year', so changing from one stylistic level, that of the written language, straightforward and syntactically logical, to that of the spoken language, which has at all times been fond of tautological constructions such as 'aujourd'hui' ('in the day of this day'), which in present-day popular French has become 'au jour d'aujourd'hui', cf. 'tout un chacun' ('un chascun' is used several times by Villon—T 596, 760, 1684, etc.), 'reculer en arrière', 'descendre en bas', etc. These constructions belong to conversation far more than to the written language, being sometimes of therapeutic value, as in the reinforcing of *hui* (<*hodie*) by the addition of 'au jour d'', but more often conveying emphasis, turning a purely intellectual statement into an affective one. It has often been pointed out that Villon's opening line is reminiscent of that of the *Roman de la Rose*: 'Ou vintieme an de mon aage' but its very word order is enough to assign it to an altogether different type of literature, popular and not courtly. It is more of a parody than a simple reminiscence.

---

[1] L. Foulet, C.F.M.A. edition of Villon's works (4th ed., 1932), p. 104; Thuasne, op. cit., vol. II, p. 77.

Que toutes mes hontes j'eus beues . . .

'boire ses hontes', 'to drink one's disgrace', 'to drain the cup of one's disgrace' is a striking metaphor, introducing the confessions straightaway on a note of intimacy and familiarity.[1]

Ne du tout fol, ne du tout sage . . .

sums up very neatly Villon's attitude towards himself, about which we are to hear so much in the following stanzas: he is not entirely foolish, and so has not deserved the harsh treatment meted out to him, but neither is he altogether wise, for he has wasted his early years and been too intent on having a good time. This line also provides the first example in the *Testament* of the use of balance and contrast, of which Villon was so fond.

> Non obstant maintes peines eues,
> Lesquelles j'ay toutes receues
> Soubz la main Thibault d'Aussigny. . . .

The way this accusation is flung out in the opening lines makes it clear that Villon is quite unable to restrain his indignation, his resentment at the way he had been treated. The very mention of the name Thibault d'Aussigny deflects him from his purpose; he switches over abruptly from describing his sufferings to vituperating against the bishop. The very suddenness of the change is in itself an indication of the strength of his feelings.

'S'evesque il est . . .' Of course he was a bishop, as Villon knew only too well. This quick remark can have only a derogatory intent: 'If bishop he is . . .' that is, 'if we really must look on him as a bishop.' '. . . seignant les rues' (literally,

---

[1] On the use of this same expression by Charles d'Orléans and other fifteenth-century poets, see S. Agada, 'Studi su Charles d'Orléans e François Villon' in *Studi Francesi*, vol. II (1960), pp. 201-19; see in particular pp. 217-19.

'signing the streets'), picturesque and pithy, is elliptical as are
so many of Villon's expressions, and Thuasne has had to
expand it considerably in his rendering: 'bénissant la foule en
faisant le signe de la croix.'[1]

'Qu'il soit le mien je le regny', the last line of the stanza,
rounds it off neatly and drives the lesson home swiftly and
surely, dispelling any shadow of doubt which may have
lingered as to his true feelings for the bishop: I deny that he is
my bishop, that is, that he has any jurisdiction over me—a
point enlarged upon in the next stanza. However, something
vital is missing from the whole of this passage. These lines
which have told us so much give us only half a sentence, less
in fact, for there is no main verb. It is of no avail hunting for
it in the second stanza, for Villon really has left his first sentence
incomplete. This appears to have been something of a mania
with him; the opening sentence of the *Lais* is also left hanging
perilously in mid-air, and if we turn to the real beginning of
the *Testament*, once the long lyrical passages of the introduction
are over, we encounter a similar feature. Here, in the burlesque
work, the traditional solemn opening of a will suddenly gives
way to a mischievous thought:

> Ou nom de Dieu, Pere eternel,
> Et du Filz que vierge parit,
> Dieu au Pere coeternel,
> Ensemble et le Saint Esperit,
> Qui sauva ce qu'Adam perit
> Et du pery pare les cieulx . . .
> Qui bien ce croit, peu ne merit,
> Gens mors estre faiz petiz dieux.   (*T* LXXX)

The construction closely resembles that of the first stanza of
the *Testament*, with an abrupt and quite unexpected switch-
over to an irreverent remark in the last two lines. One has

---

[1] op. cit., vol. II, p. 82

the impression of listening to the poet as the thoughts pass quickly through his head and he gives them their first expression, imperfect, illogical perhaps to anyone preoccupied with grammar, yet clear and natural. We follow the workings of his lively mind moment by moment. We are with him as he composes, we are at his elbow, we feel the impact of his newly formed thoughts, addressed directly, so it seems, to us. He appears to write as he would think and speak. At times the chain of thought is pushed into the background, and a mischievous aside, which slid suddenly into his mind, comes to the fore. He develops it, plays around with it, then tiring of it, drops it and reverts to his main theme, the making of his will, but it is not long before we are off once more on another digression. The internal structure of stanza after stanza, passage after passage, reflects the disjointed nature of the *Testament* as a whole. Sometimes the aside is only very brief, but then it is often the more telling, as when the old harlot warns the young ones who have taken her place that when they too have aged, they will find that nobody is interested in them any more, except old priests (*T* 547).

This cruel, biting wit, this mind hopping swiftly and dexterously from one thought to another, are traits which the French people still possess, but none has ever been able to display them to better effect than Villon, not even the seventeenth-century master of this style, La Fontaine. Villon had an advantage in that he was not compelled to be explicit and grammatically logical as is the modern French writer. He did not have to trick out his sentences with an orderly array of tool-words: conjunctions, pronouns, prepositions and the like. He shapes language to his thoughts and feelings, and if a sentence is broken off suddenly, that is of no importance, for the moment he has said what he has to say, or hinted at it sufficiently, he has already passed on to the next thought crowding into his head. This moment-by-moment way of composing determines some of the salient features of his poetry: its rambling nature, full of digressions and contrary sentiments, 'mes lubres sentemens' as he calls them. We are promised the real beginning of the *Testament* after we have read not far from 800 lines, but yet another digression intervenes, and we are kept waiting for another 50 lines or so, a wait which can be borne patiently, moreover, for the digressions have a much greater interest—for the modern reader at least—than the actual string of legacies. However, it is only too easy to use terms such as 'spontaneity' in connection with Villon, and the fact that these three beginnings, that of the *Lais*, that of the introduction to the *Testament* and that of the *Testament* proper, are construed, or misconstrued, in this way, suggests deliberate intention. The beginning of the *Lais* gives the game away even more than does that of the *Testament*. In the latter the mention of the bishop's name arouses Villon's indignation to such an extent that he is impelled to abandon his first subject in order to inveigh against the bishop, so that the change here is very clearly motivated, but in the *Lais* there is nothing to jolt him out of his first train of thought. It is simply a matter of a loosely constructed sentence which has become too involved, so necessitating a new beginning in the second stanza:

> L'an quatre cens cinquante six,
> Je, Françoys Villon, escollier,
> Considerant, de sens rassis,
> Le frain aux dens, franc au collier,
> Qu'on doit ses œuvres conseillier,
> Comme Vegece le raconte,
> Sage Rommain, grant conseillier,
> Ou autrement on se mesconte . . .

84

En ce temps que j'ay dit devant,
Sur le Noel, morte saison,
Que les loups se vivent du vent
Et qu'on se tient en sa maison,
Pour le frimas, pres du tison,
Me vint ung vouloir de brisier
La tres amoureuse prison
Qui souloit mon cuer debrisier.   (*L* I-II)

Here no suddenly occurring thought or overpowering emotion
obliges him to leave the first stanza incomplete, and he could
so easily have completed it had he so desired. This is in fact a
conscious art, not the purely undisciplined outpouring it
appears, on the surface, to be. These incomplete openings and
quick asides, like the very word order of the first line of the
Testament, declare his intention of avoiding altogether a
logically developed presentation, but this is no less an art than
any other. To write as one speaks and thinks is far more
difficult than may seem. To manage it at all is a rare achievement, and to manage it in rhymed verse of eight syllables in
such a way as to make the arguments and feelings more, not
less, forceful and convincing, is an even more formidable
achievement. It is admittedly an art well suited to Villon,
reflecting the nature of the man's mind, mercurial, penetrating,
seeing all at a glance yet unable to concentrate for long on any
one subject. It is an admirable expression of his personality,
and the art can never be wholly separated from the man. The
longest piece that we have from him devoted entirely to a
single topic and avoiding digressions of all kinds is the *Épître
à Marie d'Orléans*, which contains a mere 132 octosyllabic lines.
On two occasions Villon pretends that the *Testament* has been
dictated by him to a clerk. This is doubtless a fiction, but it is
a fiction well suited to the character of his work, suggesting
that he himself never set pen to paper. But we must not allow

ourselves to be deceived into thinking that this is all 'spontaneous', 'inspired' verse, where instinct replaces art, composed at tremendous speed in one or two days, and without effort of any kind. It has been maintained that art is the last word to use in connection with Villon. On the contrary it should surely be the first word, for writing in analogical, conversational style is an art in itself as rare in the age of the *Grands Rhétoriqueurs* as it is today. It is this art which gives his poetry its flavour and individuality, and makes it live as though he were there before our eyes, speaking directly to us.

Villon's syntax reveals to us not only the workings of his mind, but also the seeing quality of his eye, for with a few terse expressions he depicts a whole scene, imparting a photographic impression. He may mention only one or two seemingly incidental details, but they are chosen in such a way that the imagination is fired and the picture leaps into life. Here is a group of Parisiennes chatting busily together:

> Regarde m'en deux, trois, assises
> Sur le bas du ply de leurs robes,
> En ces moustiers, en ces eglises;
> Tire toy pres, et ne te hobes;
> Tu trouveras la que Macrobes
> Oncques ne fist tels jugemens. . . . (*T* 1543-8)

The *Ballade de Mercy* at the end of the *Testament* is addressed to the many types of people with whom he had rubbed shoulders in the streets of Paris; the crowds he had known and loved live and move again in this most vivid of verse:

> A Chartreux et a Celestins,
> A Mendians et a Devotes,
> A musars et claquepatins,
> A servans et filles mignotes
> Portans surcotz et justes cotes,
> A cuidereaux d'amours transsis

86

Chaussans sans meshaing fauves botes,
Je crie a toutes gens mercis.

A filletes monstrans tetins
Pour avoir plus largement d'ostes,
A ribleurs, mouveurs de hutins,
A bateleurs, traynans marmotes,
A folz, folles, a sotz et sotes,
Qui s'en vont siflant six a six,
A vecyes et mariotes,
Je crie a toutes gens mercis. . . .   (*T* 1968-83)[1]

Villon is an adept at finding the expression or adjective
which really describes and is not used merely to fill out the
line. Lote has condemned the feeble choice of adjectives in so
much medieval poetry. *Grant, bel* and such words are grossly
overworked, just as *nice* is overworked in English; descriptions
of castles, heroines, landscapes abound but they are all so stereotyped, so conventional in this age when no high store was set
by originality. Villon is one of the few poets of his century
who possess a real talent for observing directly through their
own eyes, not through those of a rather effete literature. Lote
acknowledges Villon's superiority in this respect, and quotes
the following stanza describing the harlot in her old age.
The italics are his:

Le front ridé, les cheveux gris,
Les sourcilz *cheus*, les yeulx estains,
Qui faisoient regars et ris
Dont mains meschans furent attains;
Nez courbes de beaulté loingtains,
Oreilles pendantes, moussues,
Le vis pally, mort et *destains,*
Menton froncé, levres *peaussues* . . .   (*T* LIV)

---

[1] cf. the portrait of the money-lender in *T* 1300-5, or that of Villon
sitting at his desk in the depths of winter (*L* 308-12).

Editors of Villon's poetry sometimes quote, in their notes, expressions which seem to them to refer to something that Villon has seen and of which he has kept a keen impression. Thus Thuasne, commenting on the line:

> S'evesque il est, seignant les rues . . .   (*T* 7)

suggests that before his arrest, Villon must actually have seen the bishop blessing the crowds in the streets of Orléans. G. Atkinson, commenting on the image in the following lines:

> Mes jours s'en sont allez errant
> Comme, dit Job, d'une touaille
> Font les filetz, quant tisserant
> En son poing tient ardente paille . . .   (*T* 217-20)

points out that it is a paraphrase of Job vii, 6: 'My days are swifter than a weaver's shuttle . . .', and adds: 'Villon's image is much more specific than the Biblical picture. He had *seen* the process of weaving.'[1] The substitution of a precise image for a more general one is significant, as also is the knowledge revealed here and on a number of occasions of the exact nature of the work done by people of a variety of trades and of the terms they used (cf. *T* 1103, 1713, etc., and Atkinson's remarks, op. cit., pp. 14-15). The sharp visual impact of his phraseology constantly surprises the reader and keeps him alert. On the other hand, it must be confessed that the imagination of some readers is rather too easily aroused. The mere line:

> L'emperieres au poing dorez   (*T* 394)

conjures up the whole Orient for D. B. Wyndham Lewis: '. . . the minarets; the coloured domes; the Liturgy of Chrysostom; the *ikonostasis* and its array of strange framed oval-faced saints with hands and vestments of solid gold and silver,

---

[1] *The Works of François Villon* (London, 1930), p. 250

studded with gems; the flowery Greek rites.'[1] Such effusions can be tremendous fun to read, but they are of course concerned much more with the critic's imagination than with the poetry he is supposed to be writing about. The critic's business is with the text, but to dictate exactly how the imagination should react to the poetry, or to catalogue the images which he feels it ought to conjure up, is to say the least a vain enterprise.

Brevity is the soul of Villon's genius (but not that of his critics, it would seem). Reading through his poetry one frequently comes across examples of elliptical syntax, a peculiar telescoped style which, though not representing a complete departure from the fifteenth-century norm, is used far more consistently by him than by his contemporaries, many of whose works are extremely prolix and would have benefited greatly from a more concentrated expression. It is the same with details of syntax as with his thoughts and feelings: the beginning is there, but the end is not infrequently missing. 'Qui plus est' ('moreover') becomes 'Qui plus'. 'Somme toute' becomes 'Somme' (more common in the sixteenth century than in the fifteenth). His stanzas are based on a climactic pattern which we have already encountered in the introduction to the *Testament*. The last line rounds the whole thing off and drives the point home. In this he is really following the tradition of concluding a stanza with a proverb, but he will generally substitute for the proverb a cutting expression of his own, again elliptical or paratactic in structure. Thus, having appointed his heirs who are to meet his debts and make sure that his legacies are distributed, he concludes in this way:

> De moy, dictes que je leur mande,
> Ont eu jusqu'au lit ou je gis.   (*T* 775-6)

[1] *François Villon, A Documented Survey* (London, 1928), p. 243

This brisk culmination snaps one's breath away its with very suddenness. It explains with a wry humour why these people have been chosen as heirs. The hearty, ribald laughter of the tavern echoes in this line. Another example: having bequeathed to one Mademoiselle de Bruyères the right to preach out-of-doors, Villon concludes the stanza with this stipulation:

> Mais que ce soit hors cymetieres,
> Trop bien au Marchié au fillé.   (*T* 1513-14)

The last line shows the real point of this legacy, so far quite innocuous in appearance: at the Threadmarket adjoining the cemetery will be a suitable place for her preaching, since it was there, as everyone knew, that the prostitutes were to be found.

Describing a shed or hovel in which he took refuge at one time and where he seems to have put up a hook in lieu of a sign, Villon concludes:

> Qui que l'ait prins, point ne m'en loue:
> Sanglante nuyt et bas chevet!   (*T* 1004-5)

Once more the last line is elliptical and has to be expanded in translation as have so many of Villon's lines: 'he certainly spent a beastly night in the place and had a low pillow' (i.e. slept on the ground).

Villon says what he has to say quickly, briefly, without undue wordiness, and the forceful impact of his verse is due largely to this habit. He captures beautifully the incomplete, untidy utterances of conversation. Indeed, on numerous occasions he deliberately turns his poetry into a conversation by inventing an interlocutor who objects to a statement he has just made; he then proceeds to demolish that objection, sometimes in a few lines (*T* III, LXXI, CXXXV), sometimes taking two or more stanzas (*T* LVIII-LXIV, LXXXII-LXXXIII): 'And if anyone should take me up on this . . .' (*T* 17), 'And if anyone should question me on this . . .' (*T* 725), 'And should anyone blame me for these words . . .' (*T* 571-2), 'If anyone asks me . . .' (*T* 809). He also addresses an imaginary audience (*T* XLIII, CLVI-CLVIII, CLIX, *T* 1692-1719, *T* 1968-95), sometimes adopting for this purpose a disguise such as that of the Belle Heaulmière, or else he anticipates objections and accusations as though following the line of thought his poetry creates in the reader (*T* 105-6, 185-92). He is particularly fond of poking questions at himself and then providing the answer, which may be anything in length from a couple of words to a couple of stanzas (*T* 174-6, 205-8, 225-48, 289-92, 327-8, 418-20, 609-12, 732-6, 759-60, 773-6, 914-17, 1100-1, 1283, 1355-61, 1655, 1737-43, 1815-16, 1919, 1930-2, 1934). Some of these questions are obviously supposed to come from his clerk, Firmin; for example, when he is appointing the various executors of the will, he gives their names in reply to his clerk's questions:

> Qui sera l'autre? G'y pensoye:
> Ce sera sire Colombel . . .   (*T* 1930-1; cf. 1919, 1934)

It may well be that this clerk fulfilled a need felt by Villon for another presence, someone, even if only imaginary, at whom he could fling his sarcasms and reflections. It is also worth noting that one of the longer digressions in the early part of the *Testament* takes the form of a conversation between Alexander and Diomedes, with whom Villon identifies himself: he is a Diomedes who has never met his Alexander. This conversational style is in fact one of Villon's main methods of keeping his mind on the move from one idea or feeling to another; repartee, questions, objections, accusations act as a stimulus, constantly urging him on. The conversational nature of his style is reflected also in the use of exclamatory expressions such as 'Voire' and 'Dieu merci', which appear, on the surface, merely to fill the line out, though they are not out of place in this most lyric of poetry, subjective in thought and construction alike, and are in fact reflections of the particular art of Villon.

★

In medieval French, word order was far more of a stylistic device than it is nowadays. Examples of its use to provide stress abound in the earliest texts:

> Halt sunt li pui e tenebrus e grant

in the *Chanson de Roland* (l. 1830) emphasises the height of the hills more than would 'Li pui sunt halt . . .', and also gives a more strongly marked caesura. Similarly:

> Granz est la noise, si l'oïrent Franceis   (l. 1005)

rather than 'La noise est granz . . .' stresses the loudness of the noise of battle.[1] From late medieval French onwards, word order was to become more stereotyped, but even so the fifteenth-century writer still had far more choice in such matters than has his modern counterpart. However, in any study of this subject as it affects poetry, two factors must be constantly borne in mind. Firstly, certain word orders may appear to be based on stylistic considerations but are in fact due to the exigencies of rhyme or metre. Thus, when Villon writes:

> Pour ce que foible je me sens   (*T* 73)

foible may appear to be thrown into prominence, but the placing of the word at the end of the line would not give him the rhyme he was seeking. Also, it cannot be said that he wrote:

> S'evesque il est, seignant les rues   (*T* 7)

---

[1] For other examples from the *Chanson de Roland*, see F. Brunot and C. Bruneau, op. cit., pp. 489-90.

as a more emphatic form of 'S'il est evesque . . .', for this order would involve a syllable too many, so that in point of fact he had no choice in the matter. Similarly:

> Trop forte elle est pour telz enfans   (T 1293)

would involve a syllable too many if written as 'Elle est trop forte . . .', and in the line:

> Vostre je suis et non plus mien   (PD VIII, 86)

the first word certainly seems to be singled out for emphasis, but

> Je suis vostre et non plus mien

would lack a syllable. Secondly, despite the freedom of choice open to the medieval writer in the sphere of word order, certain tendencies were followed from the earliest times. One was to place the past participle in front of its auxiliary. The *Testament* provides several instances:

> Peu [nourri] m'a d'une petite miche
>   (T 13)—not 'M'a peu . . .'

> Escript l'ay l'an soixante et ung . . .   (T 81)

> Allé s'en est et je demeure . . .   (T 177)

> Tollu m'as la haulte franchise . . .   (T 461)

> Abusé m'a et fait entendre . . .   (T 689)

> Degeté m'a de maint bouillon . . .   (T 853)

Villon was not influenced in such cases by the tendency of earlier medieval French to avoid using the regime form of the weak personal pronoun at the beginning of a line, since he writes:

> Me vint ung vouloir de brisier . . .   (L 14)

not 'Ung vouloir me vint . . .' and between them the two
testaments contain a number of such examples (*L* 28; *T* 95,
101, 148, 197, 327, 483, 996, 1010, 1413, 1480, 1592, 1675,
1773, 2015). On the other hand, this habit of inverting
participle and auxiliary was allied to the long-established one
of keeping a central position for the verb. Where a compound
tense was involved, or a construction with an infinitive, it was
the part of the verb indicating the person that was allotted the
central position; usually it was made the second element of
the sentence (cf. inversion of subject and verb after certain
adverbs in modern French, and even after conjunctions such
as *et* in Middle French), occasionally the third. Thus, for 'You
are his master', Villon could not write 'Es son seigneur'.
Theoretically he had the choice between 'Tu es son seigneur'
as in modern French, or 'Son seigneur es', but the 4-6 division
of decasyllabic verse made the former impossible and it is
accordingly the latter he has used:

> Son seigneur es, et te tiens son varlet   (*PD* XI, 34)

This order was dictated by a combination of syntactic convention and metrical requirements, not simply by a desire to
lay emphasis on *seigneur*. There is a number of similar examples in Villon's poetry:

> Mon seigneur n'est ne mon evesque . . .   (*T* 9)

> Riens ne hayt que perseverance . . .   (*T* 104)

> Griefz ne faiz a jeunes n'a vieulx . . .   (*T* 125)

> Bons vins ont, souvent embrochiez . . .   (*T* 249)

> Moue ne fait qui ne desplaise . . .   (*T* 440)

> Rondement ayment toute gent . . . (*T* 579; cf. *T* 717, 749,
> 758, 767, 801, 869, 895, 985, etc.)

Only rarely does one find a verb, positive or negative, as the first element of a line in Villon's poetry, unless it is an interrogative form, an imperative, a subjunctive expressing a hypothesis, or unless it completes a clause or sentence begun in the preceding lines:

> Moy, povre mercerot de Renes,
> *Mourray* je pas? (*T* 417-18)

> Dieu, qui les pelerins d'Esmaus
> *Conforta* . . . (*T* 99-100)

> . . . en grant povreté . . .
> Ne *gist* pas grant loyauté. (*T* 150-2)

> Griefz ne faiz a jeunes n'a vieulx
> *Soie* sur piez ou soie en biere . . . (*T* 125-6)

> *Excusez* moy aucunement . . . (*T* 149)

Of a total of over a hundred examples (a hundred positive, fourteen negative) which occur in the two testaments, only two do not fit in to any of the above categories, and even here the subject has already been given in the preceding lines:

> Ont eu jusqu'au lit ou je gis; (*T* 776)

We have seen above that this line was intended to have a startling effect.

> Regrete huy sa mort et hier. (*T* 431)

Foulet points out in the notes to his edition of Villon's poetry that this line is peculiar since it makes *hier* dissyllabic 'malgré l'usage constant de l'ancien français'.[1] He draws attention to the reading of one manuscript (F): 'Regretant sa mort huy et

[1] p. 109

95

hier', and this may well have been the original version, since the present participle, like the past participle, is frequently used by Villon at the beginning of a line.

Two questions arise from what precedes. The first is this: is word order in Villon's poetry ever influenced by stylistic considerations? The answer is certainly yes, and in more ways than one. We have already seen in the preceding chapter that euphony was an important consideration with him, and he avoids, where possible, awkward clashes of sounds. Thus, although he writes in *PD* IX, 17: 'Quant mort sera', he does not follow the same order in *T* 1760: 'Or mors sont ilz ...' but prefers: 'Or sont ilz mors ...' (also in *T* 485: 'Or est il mort...'). Similarly in *T* 11 he writes: 'Foy ne luy doy ...', not 'Ne luy doy foy ...'; and in *T* 259: 'Je ne suis juge ...', not 'Juge je ne suis'. Balance and contrast are also important considerations; thus he does not write:

> ... Quant des cuisses
> Plus ne sont cuisses, mais cuissetes.

but

> ... Quant des cuisses
> Cuisses ne sont plus, mais cuissetes.   (*T* 523)

In addition, word order is used on occasion for purposes of emphasis, as in the numerous examples of overflow mentioned earlier. Also, it is noteworthy that, when speaking of poverty and the terrible hold it had on his life, he writes, not:

> Je suis povre de ma jeunesse

but

> Povre je suis de ma jeunesse ...   (*T* 273)

But on the other hand, presenting himself as a sinner, without wishing to stress the fact any too heavily, he writes, not:

> Pecheur je suis, je le sçay bien

but

> Je suis pecheur, je le sçay bien,   (*T* 105)

and the 'je le sçay bien' makes it quite clear that he feels no need for stress: 'the fact is quite obvious enough' is the implication. In his version of the *carpe diem* theme, stressing the folly of neglecting the joys of life until one is too old to appreciate them, he writes:

> Viel je seray; vous, laide, sans couleur   (*T* 962)

not

> Je seray viel . . .

whilst in the *Ballade pour prier Nostre Dame*, which he wrote for his mother, she is made to say, not:

> Je suis femme povrette et ancïenne,

which would be a dull statement of fact devoid of emotive content, but

> Femme je suis, povrette et ancïenne,   (*T* 893)

a word order which has also the effect of giving a more firmly marked caesura, although the lyric caesura that 'Je suis femme . . .' would entail is common enough in Villon's decasyllabic verse as we have seen.[1]

This brings us to the second question arising from these remarks on word order. Is it possible, and is it necessary, to distinguish between those instances where word order was intended by the poet to achieve a stylistic effect and those where grammatical conventions or metrical requirements give the reader an impression of stylistic effect, as in

> Son seigneur es, et te tiens son varlet

[1] See above, pp. 51-2

97

The value of linguistic analysis of the type given above is that it enables us to get the poetry into a fairly true perspective. It throws light on the circumstances governing its composition, and prevents us from attributing to the poet what belonged to the period as a whole. Obviously, however, such considerations cannot be allowed to come between the poetry and our appreciation of it. We cannot postpone our reaction until the analysis has been made, as though it were some sort of post-mortem examination. Stylistic effects sometimes derive not so much from the poet's intentions as from the metre he is using and the syntactic conventions he is following. They are thus inherent qualities of the system as a whole, but are no less real for that. Furthermore the stature of the poet is revealed when the effect of his poetry is enhanced by such matters as metre and rhyme, for this is by no means an inevitable oc-currence. With lesser poets a line of verse is so often distorted, or allowed to fall flat, or to strain the understanding simply in order to achieve a suitable rhyme or the required number of syllables. There is very little straining of this kind with Villon; he is the complete master of his versification, and where he himself is not directly responsible for a stylistic effect, always and inevitably he is indirectly responsible. Thus if he had no choice between

Tu es son seigneur et te tiens son varlet

and

Son seigneur es et te tiens son varlet

he could on the other hand have chosen between the latter and

Tu es son maistre et te tiens son varlet[1]

[1] cf. *PD* III, 11 for the contrast between *maistre* and *varlet* in the same line, and *PD* V, 8 for the elision of -*e* in hiatus after the caesura (cf. above, p. 51).

so that the wording as it stands does all the same involve a choice, as any line of poetry is ultimately bound to do, be the choice felicitous or otherwise. It is not simply a matter of some effects being accidental, and therefore spurious, and others deliberate, and therefore genuine. Whether the ultimate source is provided by the personal style of the poet himself or by the language of the period in which he is writing, each trait contributes towards the impression created by the whole. The flavour of any work is in part that of its period.

*

Not the least remarkable aspect of Villon's poetry is the very wide range of vocabulary it reveals. He handles words and phrases with an exuberance worthy of a writer of the Renaissance. He revels in the word matter for its own sake. His piling up of words in crisp, staccato formation contributes to the lilt and energy of his verse. The few doublets and *clichés* apart, each word is there with a purpose and has something to add to the overall pattern. The personality the poetry builds up for itself is thin, wiry, sharp of look and quick of manner. It has none of the rather dreary obesity characterising many a late medieval poet, such as Guillaume Alexis. All is grist to Villon's mill, whether it be names of chemicals or foods, lists of proverbs or occupations, dialect forms, thieves' slang, nationalities, names of heroes or heroines, whores and harlots. We may turn to the *Ballade de Bonne Doctrine* with its argot terms, its heaping up of nouns and verbs relating to a variety of professions, most of them of a dubious kind:

> Car ou soies porteur de bulles,
> Pipeur ou hasardeur de dez,
> Tailleur de faulx coings et te brusles
> Comme ceulx qui sont eschaudez,

Traistres parjurs, de foy vuidez;
Soies larron, ravis ou pilles:
Ou en va l'acquest, que cuidez?
Tout aux tavernes et aux filles.

Ryme, raille, cymballe, luttes,
Comme fol, fainctif, eshontez;
Farce, broulle, joue des fleustes;
Fais, es villes et es citez,
Farces, jeux et moralitez;
Gaigne au berlanc, au glic, aux quilles:
Aussi bien va, or escoutez!
Tout aux tavernes et aux filles.   (*T* 1692-1707)

The raciness and vigour of these lines are quite clear to any
reader, even if the meaning is not. We may also turn to the
Ballade des Langues Envieuses which lists a wide variety of
substances in which, says Villon, certain jealous tongues should
be fried; along with several minerals he places in this witches'
brew the most loathsome things his extremely fertile mind
could conjure up. These tongues have evidently done him
harm in the past, but however fierce and nasty they may have
been, they were clearly no match for Villon's pen:

En realgar, en arcenic rochier,
En orpiment, en salpestre et chaulx vive,
En plomb boullant pour mieulx les esmorchier,
En suye et poix destrempez de lessive
Faicte d'estrons et de pissat de juifve,
En lavailles de jambes a meseaulx,
En racleure de piez et viels houseaulx,
En sang d'aspic et drogues venimeuses,
En fiel de loups, de regnars et blereaulx,
Soient frittes ces langues envieuses!   (*T* 1422-31)

An enumeration of a very different kind appears at the end of
the *Lais*, which pokes fun at the pompous language of the
Sorbonne:

> Lors je sentis dame Memoire
> Respondre et mectre en son aulmoire
> Ses especes collateralles,
> Oppinative faulce et voire,
> Et autres intellectualles,
>
> Et mesmement l'estimative,
> Par quoy prospective nous vient,
> Similative, formative . . .   (L 284-91)

The *Ballade des Proverbes* accumulates popular sayings of the day:

> Tant grate chievre que mal gist,
> Tant va le pot a l'eaue qu'il brise,
> Tant chauffe on le fer qu'il rougist,
> Tant le maille on qu'il se debrise,
> Tant vault l'homme comme on le prise,
> Tant s'eslongne il qu'il n'en souvient,
> Tant mauvais est qu'on le desprise,
> Tant crie l'on Noel qu'il vient.   (PD II, 1-8)

In the *Ballades en Jargon*, Villon takes an obvious delight in handling the special, secret language of the Parisian underworld of his day, not to be confused with argot which, unlike the jargon or *jobelin*, did not necessarily strive to place itself beyond the comprehension of all but the initiated:

> Brouez, Benards, eschecquez a la saulve,
> Car escornez vous estes a la roue;
> Fourbe, joncheur, chascun de vous se saulve:
> Eschec, eschec, coquille si s'en broue!
> Cornette court: nul planteur ne s'i joue.
> Qui est en plant, en ce coffre joyeulx,
> Pour ses raisons il a, ains qu'il s'escroue,
> Jonc verdoiant, havre du marieulx![1]

[1] Quoted from P. Champion's edition of the *Ballades en Jargon* in *Les Sources de l'argot ancien*, by L. Sainéan, vol. I (Paris, 1912), p. 136. Eleven of

This accumulative technique is an integral part of Villon's poetry, and appears throughout his work, in the lines on death, in the lists of foodstuffs, in the names of the heroes and heroines of the past, in the description of woman's beauty. It is used in various ways, sometimes merely facetiously, the better to bring out the point of a joke, sometimes more seriously, to underline the inevitability of fate, and sometimes with a bewildering mixture of the two, which imparts the cynicism to poems such as the *Ballade de Bonne Doctrine*. But this very technique reveals the fascination that Villon finds in words. He never tires of building them up into fantastic patterns. None the less, however brilliantly he uses this technique, it is far from being original. Similar features appear already in the *Chanson de Roland* and other *chansons de geste*, where poets revel in accumulating sonorous, mouth-filling words, for example in descriptions of armies:

> Li amiralz ·x· escheles ajusted.
> La premere est des jaianz de Malpruse,
> L'altre est de Hums e la terce de Hungres,
> E la quarte est de Baldise la lunge
> E la quinte est de cels de Val Penuse
> E la siste est de . . . Maruse
> E la sedme est de Leus e d'Astrimonies,

these poems are extant, but the authorship of four at least is in doubt (see K. Sneyders de Vogel, 'Les Ballades en Jargon du manuscrit de Stockholm' in *Neophilologus*, vol. I (1916), p. 69). Those which can be attributed with some certainty to Villon have survived in only one source: six in the first printed edition of Villon's works (Levet, 1489), the remaining one in the Stockholm MS. (see Bibliography, p. 154). The Levet edition makes many mistakes in the text of the *Testament* as a comparison with the extant MSS. shows. The text of the poems in jargon is certainly equally unreliable if not more so in view of the esoteric nature of the language, and here no collation with the MSS. is possible. Likewise, the Stockholm MS. is demonstrably unreliable in its transcription of various of Villon's poems. For these reasons, and also because the jargon still retains many of its secrets, this aspect of Villon's poetry is not extensively covered in the present work, although some of the more easily identifiable terms are included, cf. below, pp. 105-9.

L'oidme est d'Argoilles e la noefme de Clarbone
E la disme est des barbez de Fronde . . .[1]

According to Leo Spitzer, names have a poetry of their own, for they are less ringed about with grammatical considerations than are other words, and in consequence exist more as sounds which appeal to our ears. He quotes as example Racine's

La fille de Minos et de Pasiphaé

and then applies his remarks to Villon's accumulation of names in the *Ballade des Dames du Temps Jadis*.[2] Whatever its potentialities, this word-building technique inevitably lends itself to abuse, and the poets of the fourteenth and fifteenth centuries often overworked it, using it sometimes for no purpose other than to provide intricate leonine rhymes, or even simply to fill out a poem. With Villon it is never the case of a string of words or names serving merely as padding; always there is a motive, and always a rhythm and sound pattern appropriate to the context.

An outstanding feature of Villon's vocabulary, apart from its breadth, is its 'modernism'. Rather more than one hundred of the words he uses were, at the most, little over a century old; several old words appear in new forms unknown to writers of earlier centuries and which are still those of today; whilst about thirty which have come down to modern French appear in his poetry for the first time or were used only very rarely by his predecessors. A few others appear to have been invented by him, either in their actual form, or in the meaning and use allotted to them. The hundred or so words from the immediate past are mostly Latinisms and learned forms introduced into the language from the fourteenth century onwards.

[1] *La Chanson de Roland*, ed. F. Whitehead (Oxford, 2nd ed., 1947), Laisse CCXL on p. 95.   [2] op. cit., pp. 14-15

It is characteristic of the many-sided and contradictory nature of this poet that, having pointed out how his syntax resembles that of ordinary speech, we should have to go on to speak about his use of Latinisms. To be sure, his language is not invariably that of conversation; he was by no means without erudition, and was capable of a formal style, at times oddly out of place, as in the opening lines of the *Ballade pour prier Nostre Dame*. This prayer is supposed to be uttered by his mother, poor, ignorant and illiterate:

> . . . povrette et ancïenne,
> Qui riens ne sçay; oncques lettre ne lus . . . (*T* 893-4)

yet it begins in a pompous way with learned literary expressions:

> Dame du ciel, *regente terrienne,*
> *Emperiere* des *infernaux palus* . . . (*T* 873-4)

If this poem is so celebrated today it is because of its latter section where Villon, having cast aside his learning, has reverted to a simpler style, more suited both to him and to the occasion, and far more moving:

> Au moustier voy, dont suis paroissienne
> Paradis paint, ou sont harpes et lus,
> Et ung enfer ou dampnez sont boullus:
> L'ung me fait paour, l'autre joye et liesse.
> La joye avoir me fay, haulte Deesse,
> A qui pecheurs doivent tous recourir,
> Comblez de foy, sans fainte ne paresse:
> En ceste foy je vueil vivre et mourir. (*T* 895-902)

An occasional whiff of pedantry reminds us once again that his conversational style was not just simply 'spontaneous', 'natural', 'instinctive'. It is not that he was capable of this style and nothing else. He had to make a choice, and had to feel his way like any other in order to find the art best suited to his personality.

A look at some of the terms Villon may have introduced into French literature brings us back once more into contact with his more familiar style. Here are some examples of words which appear in his poetry for the first time, or are only rarely found earlier: *un tantinet* (*T* 1109), *la plupart* (*L* 117), *en effet* (*T* 587), *toutefois* (*T* 745, 805, 1217, *PD* VIII, 52), *corvée* (*T* 1031) in its extended sense of 'nuisance', 'bother', *altérer* (*L* 54) in its connection with thirst, *défaut* (*L* 59) in the sense of 'fault', and *en dépit de* (*T* 1803). There are good grounds for believing that *tantinet* originated amongst the people of Paris,[1] whilst an abbreviation such as *la plupart* for *la plus grande partie de* (in *T* 1832 Villon uses *la plus partie de*), a transformation such as *toutefois* for earlier *toutes voies* (cf. Spanish *todavía*), and extensions of meaning such as those involved in *corvée* and *altérer* all illustrate usages and developments common in speech. On the other hand, one old form used by Villon, *extrace* (*T* 274) in place of the then relatively new borrowing from Latin, *extraction*, had a popular flavour retained to this day by the spoken language which uses forms such as *administrace* for *administration*.[2]

Turning to the *Ballades en Jargon*, we find a host of strange words, and some familiar terms with new meanings. It is impossible to estimate Villon's originality in this sphere; he may well have coined some of these expressions himself, but we have no means of knowing. It is here that we encounter the first attested use of *niais* in its modern sense of 'simpleton'; formerly it had meant 'fledgling', having been derived from the noun *le nid*[3]; *blanc* was used in the same sense, as an

---

[1] See L. Sainéan, *Le Langage parisien au XIXᵉ siècle* (Paris, 1920), p. 24
[2] L. Sainéan, op. cit., p. 99
[3] See L. Sainéan, *Les Sources de l'argot ancien*, 2 vols. (Paris, 1912), vol. II,

extension of its first metaphorical meaning of 'innocent', 'in-experienced' (cf. modern *blanc bec*, which like *niais* referred originally to a young bird); *rouge* on the other hand meant 'cunning', owing to the reputation for slyness enjoyed by red-haired people; criminals whose ears had been cut off are described as having been 'circumcised of their handles'—*des ances circoncis*, which seems not inappropriate in a language whose word for head had meant originally 'earthenware pot' (*tête* < *testa*)! Several expressions are obviously ironical: *être accolé* meant 'to be hanged'; *le mariage* meant 'hanging'; *montjoye* ('Hill of Joy', originally the name given to a hill near Paris where St Denis was martyred) meant 'gibbet'; *un ange* was a hangman's assistant; *dorer* meant 'to lie', literally 'to cloak beneath a bright exterior'—a little like English 'to gild the pill'; a *vendengeur* was a thief, as was also *gagneur*, recalling the euphemistic use of 'to win' in modern English. *Ne pas sçavoir oignons peller* may have had the same meaning as English 'not to know one's onions'; *babiller*, originally 'to stutter' (onomatopoeic, cf. English 'to babble') meant 'to spill the beans'; *rebigner*, originally 'to squint', meant 'to look at', 'to take a squint at'; while *pigeon*, yet another word for 'simpleton', recalls an American use of the word. *Beffleur*, 'a cheat', 'swindler', is of the same origin as English 'to baffle'; *estre sur les joncs*, meaning 'to be in prison', the floor of which was covered in rushes, reveals a semantic evolution analagous to that of English 'to be on the mat'—at least they share the same basic meaning, 'to be in trouble'! Although a few of these jargon terms are obvious enough: *la dure*, 'the ground', *la tarde* (cf. modern Spanish *la tarde*) 'the evening', *le contre*, 'companion', *le coffre*, 'prison', *le banc*, 'scaffold', *le pluc*, 'spoils', literally 'peel' (cf. modern French *épluchure*), large

p. 406. The text of the *Ballades*, ed. P. Champion, is in vol. I, pp. 111-38 (see above, pp. 101-2).

numbers remain obscure and can only be guessed at.[1] Not only the meaning, but the very authorship of some of these poems is in doubt, so that one is in danger of attributing to Villon expressions which he never used in point of fact. None the less, enough is known about the poems in jargon which Villon definitely wrote, and about the jargon in general—racy, ironical, terse, absorbing expressions from a wide variety of sources—to show clearly that it had considerable influence on Villon. This is the school which fashioned his imagery, which imparted the pungency to his style and developed his feeling for words. The jargon contained special terms for even the commonest notions: some were archaic and had been forgotten by most people or had survived only in the provinces; large numbers were based on metaphorical extension of meaning; some were adopted from other languages. What the *trobar clus* had been to the troubadours of Provence the jargon was to Villon and his associates. Although the two were at opposite ends of the social scale, the *trobar clus* sophisticated, literary rather than spoken, the jargon earthy and popular, the latter was, all the same, not nearly as wholly vulgar and coarse as one might imagine. Its heterogeneous nature, by no means ignorant of learned terms and expressions, betrays people of some education, and it is known that Villon was by no means the only cleric to haunt the underworld of fifteenth-century Paris.

The influence of *jobelin* may be seen in the peculiar and original use of metaphor in Villon's poetry. It is not necessarily a matter of direct borrowing from the language of the Coquillards, but concerns rather the basic approach to words,

[1] Of the several works on the subject which have appeared since the late nineteenth century, the most complete and most informative to date is *Le Jargon de Maître François Villon* by A. Ziwès, 2 vols. (Paris, 1954; 2nd ed., Paris, 1960). There is much ingenuity in the interpretations proposed, but not all are convincing. (See Bibliography, pp. 154-5.)

a continual readiness to use even the commonest terms meta-
phorically. The reader is constantly coming across a strange
use of a word which contributes to the brisk slanginess of the
language, and helps to build up an impression of freshness, of
boundless life and vigour. The metaphor is frequently only
trifling and not necessarily original, but the cumulative effect
is considerable. Thus, in his quarrel with Grosse Margot,
Villon gives her a blow on the nose with a piece of wood:

> Dessus son nez luy en fais ung *escript*   (*T* 1609)

and in another *ballade* he refers to:

> Serpens, lesars et telz nobles *oyseaulx*   (*T* 1440)

'Beeswax' is *estrons de mouche* (*T* 1199, literally 'bees' excre-
ment'); 'physical love' is *contemplacion* when applied, mis-
chievously, to the religious Orders (*T* 1165) and more con-
ventionally *le jeu d'asne* (*T* 1566). Occasionally the meaning
of such expressions has become obscured; thus a reference to
the *caige vert* of an aged monk (*T* 1195) is generally taken to
mean his mistress, but this is uncertain; there was, apparently,
a brothel by the name of *La Caige* in the Paris of Villon's day,
and the colour green may have been associated with such
places, or may have symbolised prostitution. When Villon
wanted to say: 'What a beating I was given', he wrote in fact:
'Such mittens there were at that marriage', and it was only a
reference by Rabelais to the quaint custom of slapping people
on the back with a mitten at marriage feasts—with the idea of
implanting the occasion on their memories—that revealed the
meaning of the line. The expression appears to be unique in
medieval literature.[1] These are but a few random examples of

---

[1] A new interpretation of this passage has been put forward by A. Burger,
Lexique de la langue de Villon (Geneva-Paris, 1957), pp. 19-20, but the basic
meaning of 'Mitaines a ces nopces telles' is not affected. (The meaning of the

the peculiar metaphorical uses to which Villon puts his words. Metaphorical expressions with an altogether richer and deeper symbolical meaning occur frequently in his poetry, but these lighter, relatively insignificant ones help to create in the mind of the reader an impression of a springy, quick-fire inventiveness. Everything points to a fresh and lively mind, the very antithesis of the pedantic *Rhétoriqueurs* who ruled French poetry in the second half of the fifteenth century.

A writer of varying moods and uneven inspiration, Villon treats words in a number of ways. When facetiously inclined, he plays around with puns, using them, as he uses almost every device that language can offer, to ridicule those whom he disliked:

> Je ne suis son serf ne sa biche . . .
> > (*T* 12, *serf* = 'slave' or 'deer')
> Ne luy laisse ne cuer ne foye . . .
> > (*T* 911, *cuer* abstract or concrete)
> Qui luy laira escu ne targe . . .
> > (*T* 917, *escu* = 'coin' or 'shield')
> Qui n'entent ne mont ne vallee . . .
> > (*L* 99 *mont* = 'hill' or 'much', a variant of *mout*)

He is also fond of toying with antiphrasis in such a way that the reader never quite knows whether love means hate or black means white. At times the joke, such as it is, is plain enough:

> Et s'aucun, dont n'ay congnoissance
> Estoit allé de mort a vie . . .   (*T* 1860-1)

Villon is evidently looking on earthly life as death, and on life in the next world as true life. Sometimes a remark was for

passage, according to Burger, is 'May Noel, the third who was there, receive a beating similar to the one I had', *est* being interpreted as a copyist's error for *ait*.)

long taken at its face value: the reference to three poor orphans, for example, who in point of fact were, as we have
seen, rich old money-lenders well known in the Paris of Villon's
day. Sarcasm of this sort abounds in his poetry, and when
poking fun at people he excels; but on the other hand, when
he is writing out of duty, in praise of some benefactor, his
words not infrequently assume a leaden quality and he trips
up over them:

> Raison ne veult que je desacoustume,
> Et en ce vueil avec elle m'assemble,
> De vous servir, mais que m'y acoustume.   (*T* 1390-2)

These clumsy lines have not an ounce of feeling behind them.
Opinions differ as to how this *ballade*, written for the provost
Robert d'Estouteville, should be interpreted. Some claim
that it is the usual, insulting Villon, for, they say, the unfortunate provost's wife is compared to a ploughed field!
However much in character this may seem, it is not what the
poem in fact says, and we must resist the temptation to out-
Villon Villon by seeing some lubricous intention or thinly
veiled insult beneath every remark. The entire *ballade* is put
into the mouth of the provost, who is telling his wife of his
love for her, and is certainly not casting aspersions on her moral
behaviour. Villon simply makes the provost say: 'I do not
lose the seed I sow in your field since the fruit resembles me.
God ordained me to till and enrich it.' For once this is not
thinly disguised insult, but heavy-handed flattery. At the
beginning of the *Testament* the flattery of Louis XI, to whom
Villon owed his release from prison, is also clumsily worded
and in no way heralds the lyric poetry to follow. The lines:

> . . . suis, tant que mon cuer vivra,
> Tenu vers luy m'humilier,
> Ce que feray jusques il mourra.   (*T* 85-7)

are, to say the least, awkward, for they appear to mean: 'I will honour the king until he dies.' It has been suggested that *il* of the last line may refer to *cuer*, meaning in that case 'until I die',[1] which seems far more appropriate, but the fact remains that the line is ambiguous in a way that cannot have been intended. It is difficult to share Marot's regret that Villon was not a court poet; both the life and literature of court circles were altogether alien to his nature.

Villon was hopelessly lacking in inspiration when writing out of duty, or when he had nothing particular to say about his associates (which was rare) or about himself (which was even more rare). His poetry leaps to life whenever he is in sprightly mood or when he is breaking some victim on the wheel of his wit. But only when he is haunted by the fear of poverty, of suffering and death, does his poetry reach its greatest heights. At such moments his vocabulary, for all its scope and richness, becomes stark, ascetic almost. Vulgarisms and learned expressions alike are left on one side. Nothing could be simpler or more direct than:

> Freres humains qui après nous vivez,
> N'ayez les cuers contre nous endurcis . . . (*PD* XIV, 1-2)

The word content of this verse is very plain, yet such is the art of Villon that it echoes for long in the memory even after the context has faded away:

> Deux estions et n'avions qu'ung cuer . . .

> Hé! Dieu, se j'eusse estudié
> Ou temps de ma jeunesse folle . . .

> Les aucuns sont morts et roidis,
> D'eulx n'est il plus riens maintenant . . .

> Hommes, icy n'a point de mocquerie,
> Mais priez Dieu que tous nous vueille absouldre!

[1] Burger, op. cit., p. 16 (where the reading *jusques* in *T* 87 is also discussed)

CHAPTER V

Theme, Image and Symbol

THE metaphors which have been examined in the preceding
pages, though often vivid and unusual in themselves, relate
only to some isolated incident or passing reference, usually of
a facetious kind. Others of Villon's metaphors have much
greater significance, illustrating and often symbolising a
dominant theme in his poetry. Imagery of this kind, as against
the more casual use of metaphor, is no mere embellishment,
but is part of the innermost nature of the poetry and helps to
determine its particular character and its aesthetic value. To
like is to liken, it has been said, and a poet's most telling images
tend to cluster around those subjects which have had a particular meaning for him and have kindled his imagination. So
it is with Villon.

THE BEAUTY OF WOMAN

Villon's most complete portrayal of woman occurs in the
Regrets de la Belle Heaulmière. It is a lavish catalogue of detail,
admitting of no reticence, conventional enough, though
Villon is less modest than many of his contemporaries, and,
without a thought for any blushes, takes a long, unabashed
look at the naked beauty. This painting, however, is only one
side of a diptych, for, as in Jean de Meun's treatment of the
same theme, it is followed immediately by another showing

this same woman in all the shrivelled repulsiveness of old age. Nowhere does Villon celebrate the beauty of woman purely and simply for its own sake. If he dwells on it at length, it is merely to demonstrate how ephemeral it is, for this is part of the tragedy of life, and the fleeting nature of woman's beauty comes to symbolise for him all human life.

The most famous metaphor in all Villon's verse is provided by his calling the great heroines of the past 'les neiges d'antan'. It may well arouse only a condescending smile from the modern reader, to whom it has become banal through constant and often vilifying repetition, or through hackneyed, over-sentimentalised translation. Already Rabelais (being Rabelais) quotes the line without taking it any too seriously:

Mais ou sont les neiges d'antan?
C'estoit le plus grand soucy que eust Villon le poète Parisien.

Decidedly, the Renaissance had no sympathy for the melancholy side of Villon. When he laughs, Rabelais and others of the sixteenth century will laugh with him, but when he weeps, he weeps alone. In modern times this symbol has become part of common newspaper parlance, for any past glory, whether it is of a school of literature or of a football team, is liable to be referred to as 'the snows of yesteryear', Rossetti's translation having found favour. But in all fairness we must remember that it was an original image.[1] It must also be borne in mind that it was a sharper-edged, less purely sentimental metaphor then than now, since the word *antan* in Villon's day had the straightforward meaning of 'the previous year', without the wistful 'bygone days' connotation it has since acquired. It has mellowed with age. Leo Spitzer sees no reason why the word

---

[1] Leo Spitzer denies this, but has not been able to produce any earlier instance of the use of the expression in French. He has found a similar expression in medieval Hungarian, but this by itself proves nothing (op. cit., p. 13).

should not be read in this context with all its modern connotations, and rightly so,[1] but we must take care lest this fortuitous accretion of wistfulness and sentiment obscure the tinge of irony present in the second stanza of the poem[2]; nor must it mislead us into romanticising unduly over Villon. Ethereal images of this nature are the exception rather than the rule in his poetry. Even when reading this, the most gentle of Villon's poems, Hilaire Belloc's dictum should be kept in mind: 'If you desire one word to use as an antithesis to the word sentimental, use the word Villon.'[3]

More poignant, and more truly characteristic, is the imagery which follows a little later in the last stanza of the *Regrets de la Belle Heaulmière*, where the old women sit hunched up:

> Tout en ung tas comme pelotes
> A petit feu de chenevotes
> Tost allumees, tost estaintes.   (*T* 528-30)

This last line has of course a double meaning. The reference to the fire around which the old women are squatting involves a precise observation, since shove (hemp stalks) has indeed the characteristic of flaring up quickly when set alight; *chenevotes* is not merely a convenient rhyme word, but the exact term needed.[4] At the same time the line symbolises—and this is its main purpose—the swift passing of woman's beauty. Villon's most striking images are never mere literary conceits, depending on cleverness for their appeal. They are grotesque, incongruous even on occasions, but never artificial, since, like so many features of his work, they are drawn straight from life.

---

[1] See above, p. 37   [2] See below, pp. 118-19
[3] In the Preface to *François Villon, A Documented Survey*, by D. B. Wyndham Lewis (London, 1928), p. xi.
[4] The precise meaning of *chenevotes* is given by F. Lecoy in *Romania* (1957), p. 416. It is not 'brins de chanvre' as Burger states in his *Lexique*, but 'ce qui reste de la tige de la plante, quand on en a ôté la filasse'.

The mood, induced by this theme of fading beauty, quickly hardens into one of cynicism. Woman becomes ugly with age, and is soon an out-of-date coin. Let those who are young make the best of things, and have as many lovers, and make as much money as they can. 'Gather ye rosebuds . . .' is not the mood, however, for there is an underlying tenseness and despair. 'Eat, drink and be merry . . .' is a good deal nearer Villon's attitude. The sadness gives way to a cynical smile, a little forced though it may be. Does this give us an opportunity to quote another expression of Villon's, now become hackneyed through repetition: 'Je ris en pleurs' (PD VII, 6), symbol, it has been said, of the swift changes of mood which characterise him? We must take great care, for as we have seen in an earlier chapter,[1] heavy scorn has recently been poured on the importance once attached to these words, formerly regarded by many almost as a device of Villon. It is no longer fashionable to interpret his idiosyncrasies in the light of these words. They are as banal as could be, we are told, for most of the medieval lyric poets managed, like Gargantua after them, to weep with one eye and laugh with the other. They form a mere *contrevérité*, a paradox in a *ballade* composed wholly of such things. Charges such as these are not altogether justified, for in these words, 'Je ris en pleurs', and indeed in the whole *ballade* to which they belong, there is some thought, some truth. Villon is not simply stringing together paradoxes for their own sake, but is recording his feelings in face of the contrasting forces of life, the intermingling joys and sorrows; he is putting into words the contradictions he finds in life and in himself, and he succeeds in imparting a very personal, truly lyrical interpretation to this theme, originally supplied by Charles d'Orléans, author of the first line of the *ballade*: 'Je meurs de seuf auprès de la fontaine'. It is something more than

[1] See above, p. 15

115

a mere facetious play on words, and a melancholy atmosphere hangs over the whole of the poem. Hackneyed though the idea may be, most versions of it were couched in long-winded terms:

> Je ris des yeulx, et mon cueur pleure . . .

> Je chante par couverture
> Mais mieulx plourassent mi oeil . . .

> Mes yeulx pleurent ens et rient dehors . . .[1]

Villon's version is by far the most neat and the most telling: 'Entre toutes les différentes expressions qui peuvent rendre une seule de nos pensées, il n'y en a qu'une qui soit la bonne.'[2] 'Je ris en pleurs', when compared with other wordings of the same idea, can certainly be said to symbolise that vigour, that concentration of language which constitutes one of the salient features of Villon's verse. Though too facile and conveying too misleading an impression of sentimentality to be a symbol of the complete Villon (far too complex a figure to be compressed into so short a formula), it none the less sums up much of his attitude towards life, with its farce and tragedy—for life in Villon's eyes seems indeed to be compounded of the one or of the other with nothing between the two—and towards woman's beauty, so ephemeral, lovely in its youthful grace and tenderness, grotesque in old age when the thighs are wrinkled like dry sausages and the ears are hairy. There is sadness in the thought that beauty was there once, and bitterness at the thought of the mockery with which life has treated it. The expression captures very well Villon's art of drawing startling contrasts.

---

[1] For further examples see I. Siciliano, *François Villon et les thèmes poétiques du Moyen Âge* (Paris, 1934), p. 106, note 3.
[2] La Bruyère, *Caractères*, chap. I, 'Des Ouvrages de l'Esprit'

LOVE

Villon's attitude towards love is a strange mixture of ribaldry and slyness. Laugh at it, by all means. Poke fun at it and at lovers, by all means. Present himself as the poor cast-off lover, 'chassié comme ung souillon' (*T* 2005), never allowed even a spark of hope, by all means. Doubtless the numerous rueful jests at his own expense contain an element of truth. His love-life may well have been neither particularly happy nor particularly successful, but the fact is that Villon, for all his seemingly candid confessions, somehow contrives to leave us very much in the dark. The only wholly sincere remark on his love adventures is the following:

> . . . i vueil celer mes amours. (*T* 1069)

Outwardly at least, Villon had little but scorn for love, for though he may have been attracted by a woman's beauty he was repelled by her infidelity and deceit. She can make a man believe anything: that flour is ashes, that double aces are double threes, that morning is evening, an old sow a windmill. His love for Katherine de Vausselles, who kept him dangling on a string, earned him a severe thrashing; another lady-love, Marthe, treated him with contempt; his relations with Fat Margot the whore—or with the whores she represented[1]—filled even him with disgust; he seems to have enjoyed more success with his two ladies of Poitou, and it is here that he declares his intention of concealing his love. However, the very fact that there were two of them hardly encourages one to think that any depth of feeling was involved, and the reference occurs in any case in the farcical section of the *Testament*. Only occasionally does he forget to be playful or cynical on the subject, as when, in the *Lais*, he complains that his unfaithful mistress is breaking 'la vive souldure' of love

---

[1] See above, p. 58, note 1

(*L* 39), but even here an undercurrent of irony is present, and there is, as we have seen,[1] good reason to doubt whether the indifference of his lady-love was his true motive for leaving the capital; he had just taken part in the robbery of the Collège de Navarre, and there was a chance of further easy gains to be made in Angers. . . .[2]

In the *rondeau* on the death of a mistress (*T* 978-89), written, as he is careful to tell us, not for himself but for another, the life of a man deprived of his love is said to be no more real than that of a painting. Only in this little poem of twelve lines is the subject handled in an altogether open and direct fashion and with unashamed depth of feeling, revealed in one of the most moving lines Villon ever wrote:

Deux estions et n'avions qu'ung cuer.   (*T* 985)

A Charles d'Orléans may treat love in romantic fashion, with many a delicate conceit and many a dainty allegory, but Villon, poet of the city, not of the court, reveals all the coarseness of the street and tavern in his remarks. Both attitudes are mere façades, and only rarely in the one as in the other is found the expression of a true and deep feeling. Both follow conventions, but of a different kind and provenance, the one realistic, a mockery, the other romantic, an idealisation.

Villon sympathises, albeit cynically, with women, and does not blame them for taking more than one lover, since, so he says, it is in their nature to do so; but he has not a single kind remark to make about any of the women in his life, unless we take seriously the reference to the two ladies of Poitou, of whom he at least condescends to write: 'Elles sont tres belles et gentes'. Even in that supposedly ethereal poem, the *Ballade*

---

[1] See above, p. xv

[2] However, Villon may have had other, and more innocent, reasons for wanting to visit Angers (see Bibliography, p. 161).

des Dames du Temps Jadis, a note of irony creeps in the moment love becomes the subject. The second stanza celebrates two heroines of the past renowned for their passionate love:

> Ou est la tres sage Helloïs
> Pour qui chastré fut et puis moyne
> Pierre Esbaillart a Saint Denis?
> Pour son amour ot ceste essoyne.
> Semblablement, ou est la royne
> Qui commanda que Buridan
> Fust geté en ung sac en Saine?
> Mais ou sont les neiges d'antan?   (*T* 337-44)

A truly magnificent love story is that of Héloïse and Abelard, nobler and purer by far than that of the infamous Marguerite de Bourgogne and the unfortunate Jean Buridan, a fourteenth-century rector of the University of Paris (remembered nowadays more for his donkey than for his love affairs!); but, though the two legends represent opposite extremes of passion, illustrating yet again Villon's love of contrast, he hardly singles out the nobler aspects of either. He is far more concerned with the fate of the unhappy lovers than with the feelings of the ladies about whom the poem is supposed to be written. He is in danger of losing grip on his central theme (he so often is!) for he simply cannot refrain from driving the lesson home:

> Pour son amour ot ceste essoyne.   (*T* 340)

—it was love which brought him this tribulation. In his view love will always lead man to grief, and already here we are not so very far in mood from the *Double Ballade* which follows shortly and whose theme is that love brings disaster to all men. The mockery has not yet come to the fore, that is all; there is not yet the cynical smile of:

> Bien est eureux qui riens n'y a!   (*T* 632, 640, etc.)

VILLON THE DEVOUT

Villon's fierce determination to wrest what joys he could from life on earth, his feeling that, even for the poor and utterly destitute, life is still well worth while, his horror of death, may give one doubts as to his religious convictions. He was not, it is true, particularly anxious to leave this world, despite all his miseries, but it was not so much a fear of death which haunted him as a fear of dying, a fear of those dreadful last agonies on the death-bed. It was in a way those very fears that encouraged him to seek some enjoyment from life; if he could manage this at least, he would resign himself to meet his end. His last word on the subject in the *Testament* is that, so long as he has had his pleasures, the idea of dying does not displease him (*T* 420).

Villon's sincerity has been called into doubt on a variety of subjects, but no critic has ever denied the depth of feeling of a poem such as the famous *Épitaphe* with its refrain: 'Mais priez Dieu que tous nous vueille absouldre' or that of the equally famous *Ballade pour prier Nostre Dame*. An occasional reader may feel that a man of Villon's morals cannot possibly have known any sincere religious convictions. Such impressions were a good deal more common in the nineteenth century than in the more tolerant atmosphere of the twentieth, when it has become very much more difficult to 'épater le bourgeois'. However, Villon himself provides the answer to such recriminations, which may well have been levelled at him by certain men of his own day such as Thibault d'Aussigny or Guillaume de Villon:

Je suis pecheur, je le sçay bien;
Pourtant ne veult pas Dieu ma mort,
Mais convertisse et vive en bien,
Et tout autre que pechié mort.

120

Combien qu'en pechié soye mort,
Dieu vit, et sa misericorde,
Se conscience me remort,
Par sa grace pardon m'accorde.   (*T* xiv)

Villon's attitude towards the Church is a rather different matter. Although he had been brought up by a member of the Church, or perhaps because of that very fact, he reveals considerable envy of the clergy. The canon, as we shall soon see,[1] figures largely in his picture of the ideal life, but, as we might expect from Villon, it is a picture devoted entirely to physical, not spiritual matters, and he doubtless had his tongue in his cheek when he made a canon the hero of his poem. He also chooses bishops, along with magistrates, to represent all rich people of high estate (*T* clxii), and as we have seen, he leaves us in no doubt as to his feelings for the bishop who had imprisoned him, showering on him insults made all the greater by the transparent disguise which cloaks them. His real hatred he reserves, however, for the religious Orders, and he never loses an opportunity of ridiculing the monks:

S'ilz font plaisir a nos commeres
Ilz ayment ainsi leurs maris . . .   (*T* 1172-3)

Such criticisms were common already long before Villon's day, and he himself reminds us that he was not alone in making such attacks; he even records disapprovingly that one author had felt it necessary to retract:

Quoy que maistre Jehan de Poullieu
En voulsist dire *et reliqua*,
Contraint et en publique lieu,
Honteusement s'en revoqua.
Maistre Jehan de Mehun s'en moqua
De leur façon, si fist Mathieu;

[1] See below, pp. 122-3

Mais on doit honnorer ce qu'a
Honnoré l'Eglise de Dieu.   (*T* cxviii)

The last two lines, it need hardly be said, are heavily ironical. Villon in fact merely reflects the attitude of the ordinary people, who spat whenever they encountered a Dominican friar in the street. His hatred was not without a tinge of envy, for the monks lived, at least in Villon's estimate, on the fat of the land.[1]

RICH MAN, POOR MAN . . .

Villon wished to have his say in a literary debate which had occupied more than one poet over the preceding hundred years or so: which was preferable, life in the country, or life in the town? Ever devoted to his Paris, Villon had no doubt that town-life represents the true life of ease, and he sets out to symbolise his ideal in a *ballade*. His portrayal shows a fat canon beside a fire in a well-carpeted room, with his lady-love, Dame Sidoine, lying at his side; they are sipping hippocras and are both naked. We must not judge Villon too harshly as a result of the cynical undertones of this poem, since in the first place he is defending a thesis and is bent on evoking some scene which would counterbalance earlier representations of the ideal life as being one of chaste purity spent amidst simple country surroundings; and secondly he quite obviously had his tongue in his cheek in this passage as in so many others. When this has been said, the fact remains that this picture, for all its crude sensuality, is in a way representative not only of Villon's imagery but of his poetry in general, concerned so extensively with the physical life, and for ever engaged in a vain pursuit of the life of ease; there is certainly great feeling in the refrain: 'Il n'est tresor que de vivre a son aise' (*T* 1482,

---

[1] See below, p. 124

1492, etc.). He is constantly preoccupied with fine food and drink, and with love-making. To the question: what are the three best things in life? he would certainly have replied, eating, drinking and wooing. Eustache Deschamps wrote a similar poem, looking at the canon through the same peep-hole as Villon, so to speak. He takes a glance round the room, noting the gold and silverwork of the furniture, but he is much too discreet to tell us about the canon, and indeed is more interested in the furniture than in the occupants. Villon on the other hand notices only the warmth of the room, the carpet and the presence of good drink, then he positively shoulders the canon to one side, so strongly does he wish himself in his place, and devotes the rest of his attention to the lady, whose skin he strokes and caresses with his accumulated adjectives: 'Blanche, tendre, polie et attintee . . .' (*T* 1476).

Villon frequently portrays the life of the rich, and by piecing together his symbols, we realise just how sensual his conception was, and how his attitude, concerned solely with external appearances, was based on envy and longing. Riches in his eyes spelt happiness, and he would probably have disagreed violently with anyone foolhardy enough to suggest to him that the two are not indissolubly associated. The symbols of prosperity are a house and a soft bed (*T* 204), feasting and merriment (*T* 1740-1), fine clothes (*L* 122), and the right to keep a pack of hounds for hunting (*L* xvii-xviii). The womenfolk have special collars and hair styles (*T* 309-11), and exclaim 'Enne!' or 'Ennementes!' (*T* 1573 and 1580), the equivalent, roughly, of 'Really!' On the tombs of the rich, crowns and sceptres are depicted (*T* 276-80). But it is on their food that Villon dwells at such length. The rich man's fare he represents symbolically as being one of cream, frumenty and rice (*T* 1764), but he is not content to stop there, and his poetry becomes at times a veritable gastronomical guide to the rich man's table, including that of the monks. The latter he describes as being 'booted and gaitered like oyster-fishers', referring doubtless to the luxury of their lives, for they had moved far from the asceticism of the distant past, when they were barefoot or wore only sandals. They have, he says, bread and pittance enough, but he simply cannot resist devoting a whole mouth-watering stanza to the detail, showing at the same time, in his usual sarcastic manner, the true nature of the monks' pittance:

> Bons vins ont, souvent embrochiez,
> Saulces, brouetz et gros poissons,
> Tartes, flans, oefz fritz et pochiez,
> Perdus et en toutes façons.
> Pas ne ressemblent les maçons,
> Que servir fault a si grant peine:
> Ilz ne veulent nuls eschançons,
> De soy verser chascun se peine. (T XXXII)

No matter how splendid the way of life, all must die in the end, and Villon would have God pardon the rich as all others (T CLXIV)—except those who had imprisoned and tortured him. But as long as they have walked the earth he has stared at them with envious gaze and noted the luxury of their lives, of which he shows such detailed knowledge that one suspects that he must at one time have tasted luxury sufficiently to whet his appetite; perhaps when still very young and under the guardianship of Guillaume de Villon, perhaps while his pockets were still full of the proceeds of the robbery of the Collège de Navarre.

Poor though he may be, Villon claims for himself the right to have his fling, and those of humble stature like himself can have an occasional taste of the good things of life, though no luxury is involved. 'A log, some coal, and peas with bacon', is a legacy symbolising a good feast round a fire, which Villon makes to his poaching friends Loup and Cholet, and doubtless this would have gone well with their bag of a duck (L xxiv). The servants in the houses of the rich may feast well on flans and cheese-tarts once their masters are in bed, and afterwards they may indulge in love-making (T cxlvii). But the poor man's glimpses of the life of ease—and they are only glimpses at best—depend on trickery in one way or another, for it is generally a matter of outwitting the rich, as in the *Repues Franches*,[1] a farcical work of the later fifteenth century which depicts Villon as the leader of a band of rogues, a kind of Robin Hood of the streets, living on his wits.

Just as he dwells with passion on the luxurious detail of the rich man's life, so Villon is never tired of drawing the contrast and underlining the destitution of the poor, those who, as he says in a memorable line, see bread only in the windows:

Et pain ne voient qu'aux fenestres . . .   (T 236)

This picture of the ragged beggars, gazing with longing at food that is denied them, is one of the most touching symbols of poverty in all literature. The poor never eat 'figs and dates' (L 315), and doubtless he would say of them as he said of himself that they are too often starving to be able to indulge in the more pleasant things of life, for, as the proverb said, 'the dance comes from the belly' (T 200). In addition to the beggars, there are the shop-boys, the lamp-lighters, the pedlars who wear coarse common cloth and eat dry bread, while they drink only water. Old age increases the suffering and helplessness of the poor, for in old age they exist to no purpose and attract only the sneers of the young. 'There is no crop in his plum tree' is a metaphor depicting the sterile fatigue of the old jester (T 444).

[1] See above, p. xx

As we have seen, Villon would also have put the life of the peasant under this heading, but his remarks on this subject occur only in the *ballade* mentioned above, in which the contrast is drawn between town-life and country-life. He imagines the country-dweller, Franc Gontier, sleeping with Helen beneath the rose-bush and eating coarse plain food:

> De gros pain bis vivent d'orge et d'avoine . . .   (*T* 1493)

the thought of which had brought pleasure to some, though it brings only disgust to the poverty-stricken yet luxury-loving Villon (*T* 1483-1502). There may, however, be something more than mere inborn inclination in these lines, for in the period he spent away from Paris, Villon very likely had his fill of the rustic life. He declares that every bush between Paris and Roussillon (the small town near Vienne, in the Isère, not the province) had, somewhere on it, 'a shred of his petticoat' (*T* 2010), an expression symbolising in a characteristically pungent way his wanderings about the countryside in the period between the composition of the two testaments. It was one thing to write verse on the beauty of rustic life, as some of the more romantically-inclined, idealising poets had done, but quite another to live it. The rejection of romantic dreams of this sort in favour of a straightforward realistic attitude to life based on his observations and experiences is characteristic of Villon.

Many of Villon's symbols concern either extreme poverty or extreme luxury, between which his own life seems to have been divided. His attempts to find a short cut from the one to the other led to his life of dishonesty spent in and out of prisons, pushing him further and further into the morass from which he was trying to escape. Only after the 1461 imprisonment, when it was too late, did he come to acknowledge that had he been steadier and more diligent in his youth, he might himself have been numbered amongst the well-to-do. It is the fact that there is no going back on his past which imparts the poignancy to his regrets.

Villon's envy of the rich is made all the sharper by his own wretched plight, with which his most striking images are concerned. Many are caricatures, the very absurdity and grotesqueness of which must have greatly amused his companions of the street and tavern. Yet if they at times arouse a smile, it is a sympathetic one, for the portrait they draw is humble, familiar and disarming. Already in the *Lais* he describes himself as being, in appearance, 'dry and black like a flue-brush' (*L* 316), and in the *Testament* he is 'sad, disheartened, blacker than a mulberry' (*T* 179) though, as the context indicates, this last metaphor refers not so much to appearance as to mood, in which sense the expression was used by another fifteenth-century poet, Jean Régnier.[1] Elsewhere he compares his appearance to that of 'an old, worn-out cart-horse' (*T* 734). Having lost all the hair on his head as the result of a disease, he looked like 'a peeled turnip' (*T* 1897). His meagre prison fare allowed his teeth to grow 'longer than rakes' (*PD* IX, 26); his head is 'harder than a pebble' (*PD* XI, 25); his body is more vile than 'a bear or pig wallowing in mud' (*PD* XV, 28); he is 'thinner than a chimera'—a mythological animal generally depicted with protruding ribs— (*T* 828). In a moment of wisdom he saw himself looking 'like a wretched dog crouching in a corner' (*PD* XI, 5). Those who have suffered like him, and who earn his sympathy as a result, are painted, as he himself is, in grotesque fashion. The ageing jester is like an old monkey (*T* 439); the old women squatting on their haunches look like a heap of balls (*T* 528); the thighs of the old harlot are like dry sausages (*T* 524).

---

[1] *Les Fortunes et adversitez de Jean Régnier*, ed. E. Droz, S.A.T.F. (Paris, 1923), l. 1429

Finally, the most striking image of this type, the bodies of the criminals swinging on the gallows are 'more pecked by birds than is the thimble by the needle' (*PD* xiv, 28).

Grotesque images provide Villon's poetry with one of its most effective and characteristic features. They give it its *gauloiserie* and distinguish it sharply from the more polished and conventional courtly verse. They give it its roughness and humour and that element of shock which at times may only amuse, but which never fails to awaken some response; it is a poor imagination indeed which remains insensitive to Villon. The peculiarity of these images lies in the sympathy which they can command even when they make us smile. They make grotesqueness the trade-mark of misery. For all their coarseness, these images are used with balance and restraint. How unfaithful to Villon, how merely absurd, was Swinburne, when he rendered the line 'oreilles pendantes, moussues' from the description of the Belle Heaulmière in her old age, as 'foul flapping ears like water-flags'. Villon's caricatures are recognisable and convincing because they are based on his observations of life. Swinburne's are nothing but wordiness and a hankering after alliteration: they are purely literary images, with not a shred of life underlying them. They may suit the length of the line and the sound pattern he has chosen, but they are totally unconvincing as metaphors, and in no way do they add to the evocative powers of the verse.

Villon's images are indeed an integral part of his poetry, and are not mere decoration added for effect. It is true that some of his more conventional similes involve obvious comparisons, as when white wine is 'as white as chalk' (*L* 127); Blanche de Castille is, appropriately enough in so far as her name is concerned, 'white as a lily' (*T* 345); the birth-mark on the face of James II of Scotland was 'as purple as an amethyst' (*T* 367—a note of mischief here, of course); the mourners at the funeral of Villon, the martyr to love, will be dressed in clothes 'as red as vermilion' (*T* 2000). Clearly, colours do not interest him as such, neither does nature, and even the streets of Paris only incidentally. His work acquires its individuality from the visual images concerning himself and others who have lived and suffered like him. Take them away and his poetry loses not only a large part of its raciness and pungency, but much of its real meaning, for their outward grimace of farce does not conceal the inner tragedy of life.

Simile and metaphor, so says C. Day Lewis, are signs of sympathy, of love, felt by the poet for things outside himself. Villon's most striking and truly original figures of speech are reserved, not for things, but for those whose lives have been as degraded as his own, those with whom he felt completely familiar. For others, whether his mood be merry, scurrilous, angry or sad, he finds no telling metaphors. Jehan Cotart he can compare only to a good bowman because he grips his tankard firmly; Thibault d'Aussigny, Louis XI, Jacques Cuer, even his parents, Katherine de Vausselles and the other women he has loved take up a good proportion of his verse but earn no metaphors from him, unless we are to include such trivialities as 'love harder than iron to chew' (*T* 944). In this last category an exception must be made of Grosse Margot who, blown up with wind, is 'more bloated than a poisonous dung-beetle' (*T* 1612), but the exception is only apparent, for he places her on the same miserable level as himself, the only woman in his life whom he can so treat. A fine pair they make, Flue-brush and Dung-beetle! He can insult her as freely as he can insult himself, but at the same time she has his sympathy, since they are together in their degradation:

Je suis paillart, la paillarde me suit.
Lequel vault mieulx? Chascun bien s'entresuit ... (*T* 1622-3)

His images concern those for whom he could feel, as he felt for himself, pity, shame and regret; those who have been left with nothing in life but 'honte et pechié'. The psychology they reveal is most fascinating. The main subject of his lyrical verse is himself, and his keenest sympathy is reserved for those in whom he finds something of himself, as though their way of life can condone his own. The one person who has known misery like him and for whom he has an obvious affection, yet has found no telling image of a grotesque kind, is his mother; this love alone will permit of no mockery.

Villon's images never attempt to uplift or beautify, save only for the remote 'neiges d'antan', a metaphor unique in character in his verse, unique too in that it concerned people he had never known or seen. He is indeed the poet of the poor and the degraded, the wretched and the mean. His art at times recalls that of the caricaturist, Dubout, who has illustrated an edition of Villon's poetry, but at others, at its most poignant, it recalls Goya, whose faces are so often distorted by misery and torment. The strange thing is that, despite all the wretchedness with which he was only too familiar, and which he has depicted more vividly than any other medieval poet, there is about his work a tremendous zest for life, a feeling that, no matter what troubles life heaps on us, it is all well worth while:

> Mieulx vault vivre soubz gros bureau
> Povre, qu'avoir esté seigneur
> Et pourrir soubz riche tombeau.   (*T* 286-8)

CHAPTER VI

Significance and Originality

THE explanation of Villon's success with posterity is not to be sought in his themes, all of which were commonplaces in the Middle Ages. His work has been shown to be an anthology of banalities, lifted above the verse of his predecessors by 'la vie mystérieuse et magique de la poésie'.[1] Indeed on the surface there is little new in Villon. Whether it be in the idea of a mock testament, in the diatribes on the omnipotence of death, in donning the garb of a martyr to love, in the writing of a hymn to the Virgin Mary, it had all been done before: 'Tout ce que ses devanciers avaient dit, tout ce que ses contemporains disaient, Villon n'a fait que le répéter. Mais il le dit mieux, beaucoup mieux que les autres.'[2] His fame must undoubtedly be attributed largely to his style, and in the preceding pages questions of rhythm, sound patterns, syntax and imagery have been considered in an endeavour to show the truth of this. However, the end of the last chapter has brought us to something new about the spirit of Villon's poetry which deserves study over and above the question of style alone. Stylistics cannot explain everything.

*

Medieval poets were fond of listening to the sorrowings of old women recalling the past, and reflecting how they

---

[1] I. Siciliano, op. cit., p. 445   [2] I. Siciliano, ibid.

would re-arrange it, could they live it over again. Such a theme presented a wonderful opportunity to the didactic poet, who could exploit these regrets to point edifying themes for the younger generation. It must not be forgotten that a very powerful vein of didacticism runs throughout French literature from the tenth to the fifteenth centuries, owing to the tremendous influence of the Church. Other poets of a more independent nature, notably Jean de Meun, used this same theme to develop cynical ideas on life and so to attack the moral teachings of the age. Villon's version is the *Regrets de la Belle Heaulmière* in which the presentation and arrangement of the theme have certain features in common with a poem written rather less than a century earlier by Eustache Deschamps. A comparison of this work with that of Villon is instructive in the light it throws on our poet.

Deschamps's *Lay du Desert d'Amours*[1] is put into the mouth of an old woman lamenting over her past. She had been beautiful and greatly admired when young, but now is ugly and ignored; in the past many had fallen in love with her and would have gone to any lengths for her favours:

> L'un en noir son habit mue
> Pour moy; l'autre de sang sue;
> L'autre languist en tristesce;
> L'un se meurt, l'autre se blesse;
> L'un m'escript qu'amours l'argue,
> L'autre tent a ma venue
> Chançon de ma gentillesse,
> De mon bien, de ma jeunesse,
> Qui depuis m'est chier vendue.[2]

She, however, had remained faithful to one lover:

---

[1] *Œuvres*, ed. Le Marquis de Queux de Saint-Hilaire and G. Raynaud, S.A.T.F., 10 vols. (Paris, 1878-1901), vol. II, pp. 182-92.
[2] ll. 78-86

Un seul en avoie amé
    Et clamé
De cuer et de voulenté
Mon ami tressouverain;
Foy, Amour et Loyauté
    Lui porté
Et en toute humilité;
Mais j'ay travaillié en vain,
Car quant mon aage mondain
M'est un petit trespassé,
De moy s'est rendu lointain
    En desdain . . .
Mon bon temps m'a po duré
    Sy mourré
En tristesce et maleurté:
Tresdoleureuse me claim.[1]

The resemblance to Villon's poem, even in the detail, is striking; Villon's protagonist, the Belle Heaulmière, is here addressing old age:

Tollu m'as la haulte franchise
Que beaulté m'avoit ordonné
Sur clers, marchans et gens d'Eglise:
Car lors il n'estoit homme né
Qui tout le sien ne m'eust donné,
Quoy qu'il en fust des repentailles,
Mais que luy eusse habandonné
Ce que reffusent truandailles.

A maint homme l'ay reffusé
Qui n'estoit a moy grant sagesse,
Pour l'amour d'ung garson rusé,
Auquel j'en feiz grande largesse.
A qui que je feisse finesse,
Par m'ame, je l'amoye bien!
Or ne me faisoit que rudesse,
Et ne m'amoit que pour le mien.   (*T* XLVIII-XLIX)

[1] ll. 145-64

133

Both had given themselves to one man in the 'bon temps', though both had been beautiful and had attracted the attentions of many. Both seem illogical, for they regret having loved and yet look back nostalgically to the 'good old days'. However, the Belle Heaulmière had been treated harshly by her cruel and indifferent lover who had died more than thirty years earlier, apparently when they were still living together; Deschamps's heroine had been abandoned outright when her beauty had begun to wane. Henceforth the two poems draw rapidly apart. In that of Deschamps the old woman withdraws to the Desert of Love, frequented only by those who yield to 'fol amour' in their youth, and after long complaints the poem is concluded with a moral lesson:

> Garde chascune sa layne
> Des loups, que ne soit plumee,
> Ou jeune temps, et apprangne
> Comment j'ay esté menee
> Tant que ne soit ramenee
> En ce desert que j'ensaigne;
> Aime honeur et honte craingne,
> Ne soit a nul ahurtee
> Mais sa jeunesce ordonnee
> Franchement, quoy qu'il aviengne.[1]

The didacticism which concludes Deschamps's poem and is its real *raison d'être* could have come from the pen of many a medieval poet. Deschamps's faded beauty is pathetic only as long as she presents her feelings in a forthright manner. Her retirement to the Desert of Love, where her complaints are interspersed with allusions to *Vaillance, Loyauté, Vieillesse, Pitié* and *Amour*, transforms her abruptly into a ventriloquist's dummy, a mechanical mouthpiece for the didactic poet. It must not be implied that this was Deschamps's only vein; he

[1] ll. 304-13

was as capable as Jean de Meun or Villon himself of writing scurrilous verse, and elsewhere he reveals qualities of his own, but in this poem he stands, aptly enough, for a whole tradition.

The Belle Heaulmière conforms to pattern in that she too moralises:

$$\text{Que m'en reste il? Honte et pechié} \dots \qquad (T\ 484)$$

but the lesson she gives is restricted to this one line. The fact of the sin is noted, the effect it has on the mind, a lesson whose very starkness and directness make it more forceful and telling than the long-winded preaching of Eustache Deschamps. What becomes of the Belle Heaulmière? Her Desert of Love is of another kind. It is the very body of the old woman, and the tragedy lies in the ravages wrought by old age; these ravages are as grim and inevitable as the death which Villon has just depicted in the passage of the *Testament* preceding this poem. Unlike Deschamps, Villon does not for a single moment abandon the world of reality. For him and his *dramatis personae* there can never be any withdrawal from life. He keeps his personage in front of him, clearly, all the time. He feels for her and with her. Her lamentations over the withering of her body provide the main subject, and do not serve merely to provide a pretty little allegory on youth and old age. So direct and poignant are her regrets that they allow of no lengthy moral lesson. The short, quick remarks which Villon lets fall in so apparently casual a manner—'Quoy qu'il en fust des repentailles . . .' 'Que m'en reste il? Honte et pechié . . .' 'Qui n'estoit a moy grant sagesse'—reveal a psychological penetration, an intuitive understanding of human nature, an utterly convincing realism, far beyond the grasp of a Deschamps. But where is the originality in all this? 'Tout est dit, et l'on vient trop tard . . .' is the lesson we are supposed to repeat, for all this had been said before Villon's time. Just as medieval poets were never tired of describing at length and in vivid detail the beauty of a young woman, so they were never weary of describing the repulsive ugliness of old age, a contrast which appears already in the *Ars Amatoria* of Ovid:

> Tempus erit quo tu, quae nunc excludis amantes,
> Frigida deserta nocte iacebis anus,
> Nec tua frangetur nocturna ianua rixa,
> Sparsa nec invenies limina mane rosa.
> Quam cito (me miserum!) laxantur corpora rugis,
> Et perit in nitido qui fuit ore color.[1]

For so many medieval poets—Jean de Meun, Deschamps, Villon, etc.—'Naso magister erat . . .' But what lies beneath this theme, and why do the poets come back to it so often? 'L'amour du contraste, le sentiment de la vanité et de la déchéance de toute chose humaine . . .' are two reasons given by Siciliano.[2] There is also the didactic motive: beauty is only skin deep and cannot last long; one must cultivate an inner beauty and be humble, bearing in mind the transitory nature of all human things. . . . The opposite point of view, Ovid's 'carpite florem', is developed at length by *La Vieille* in Jean de Meun's section of the *Roman de la Rose*: beauty is not a very sound or stable capital, and must therefore be exploited to the full as long as it is possessed:

> Le fruit d'Amours, se fame est sage,
> Cueille en la fleur de son aage,
> Car tant pert de son tens, la lasse,
> Con sanz joïr d'amours en passe.
> E s'el ne creit ce mien conseil,
> Que pour comun profit conseil,
> Sache qu'el s'en repentira
> Quant vieillece la flestira.[3]

---

[1] *Ars Amatoria*, III ll. 69-74   [2] op. cit., p. 383
[3] ed. E. Langlois, S.A.T.F. (Paris, 1922), vol. IV, ll. 13483-90

It is on this side of the fence, eventually, that Villon places himself, in the poem which follows the *Regrets de la Belle Heaulmière*, when the old prostitute gives advice to her successors. However, we must not pass over the final stanza of the *Regrets*. The sad contemplation of her body ended, the Belle Heaulmière concludes in a fashion radically different from that of the old woman in Deschamps's poem:

> Ainsi le bon temps regretons
> Entre nous, povres vielles sotes,
> Assises bas, a crouppetons,
> Tout en ung tas comme pelotes,
> A petit feu de chenevotes
> Tost allumees, tost estaintes;
> Et jadis fusmes si mignotes! . . .
> Ainsi en prent a mains et maintes. (*T* LVI)

In this stanza the canvas is broadened; the Belle Heaulmière is joined by others. The picture of the poor old women sitting hunched around their tiny fire, already quoted for its striking imagery,[1] is vivid in the extreme, but we are not concerned here with Villon's art. These lines contain something foreign to Villon's contemporaries and predecessors, foreign also to Ovid, simple enough though it may be. It is the pathos underlying the misery of the 'povres vielles sotes'; more than that, it is the feeling that Villon himself has for the old women, a feeling so strong that he almost identifies himself with them. It is owed to the fact that his own experiences provide the starting-point for his soundings of human misery. As a poet he stands apart in order to narrate and describe, but before he does that he has seen and lived the sorrows which afflict all people. When he writes in the third person it is in the spirit of the first person, and when he writes in the first person the spirit of the third is never far away, it is all Villon, nothing but

---

[1] See above, p. 114

Villon. It is also the sum of human wretchedness; the lonely, the sick, the lovelorn, the dying, the destitute, the old and withered, the scorned and neglected, the jealous, the disillusioned, the dissolute, all are there, he has known them all, seen them all, been them all. That is why at his hands the old women are not mere stiff, wooden puppets which serve conveniently for the giving either of moral lessons, or of cynical advice, although this must come in the end. They remain living creatures. Always in Villon's poetry there is life beneath the word. The reflection of himself in others awakens an instant response:

> . . . aux povres qui n'ont de quoy,
> Comme moy, Dieu doint patience!   (*T* 245-6)

His very use of the word 'povre' is significant. It is applied several times to himself: 'le povre Villon', 'ung povre petit escollier', etc.; but also to his mother: 'ma povre mere'; to the worn-out old jester: 'povre viellart'; to the aged and abandoned prostitutes: 'povres vielles sotes'.[1]

Many a remark inspired by his own plight reaches out beyond himself:

> . . . en grant povreté
> Ne gist pas grande loyauté . . .   (*T* 150-2)

> Necessité fait gens mesprendre
> Et faim saillir le loup du bois.   (*T* 167-8)

The fact that these last two lines are an adaptation of a proverb need detract not at all from their effect. Admittedly they provide a lame excuse for misdemeanours—as Du Cerceau wrote over 200 years ago: 'Si telle patenôtre sauvoit de la

---

[1] See N. Edelman, 'A Scriptural Key to Villon's *Testament*' in *Modern Language Notes*, 1957, p. 348.

corde, il y auroit peu de gens de pendus pour vol'[1]—but this is just the sort of self-defence that many a miscreant pleads; it is so very true to life.

None can escape the horrors of death:

> Et meure Paris ou Helaine,
> Quiconques meurt, meurt a douleur . . . (*T* 313-14)

the gradual withering away of the body:

> C'est d'umaine beaulté l'issue! (*T* 517)

the sorrows of old age:

> Ainsi en prent a mains et maintes. (*T* 532)

the anguish of an unrequited love:

> C'est le droit loyer qu'amans ont:
> Toute foy y est viollee . . . (*T* 619-20)

Even in the epitaph he wrote for himself he thought of others, for when he saw himself in that dreadful vision, hanging from the gallows, a body washed by the rain and shrivelled by sun and wind, he included those who had suffered the same fate along with him, and linked all men together in one last appeal:

> Freres humains qui après nous vivez,
> N'ayez les cuers contre nous endurcis,
> Car, se pitié de nous povres avez,
> Dieu en aura plus tost de vous mercis. (*PD* xiv, 1-4)

At such moments he saw himself not so much as an individual, but as one tiny part of a vast cosmos. You can outlaw a criminal, condemn him to death, hang him, but he is still a man for all that and deserves to be thought of as such. Nobody can contract out of life, or be cut off from human destiny and cast aside altogether. He pleads for the prostitutes and is not ashamed to converse with them, for, he says, they too were

---

[1] Essay at the back of the 1723 edition of Villon's works, p. 32

139

honest to begin with; human nature has made them what they are, and there is little point in blaming them for this.

Villon's experiences have taught him that we can no more escape from life than we can from death, and that life makes us what we are: the Belle Heaulmière, symbol of all human misery, is not responsible for her degradation. Literary experience and intellectual arguments take second place, and almost as significant as what is present in Villon's poetry is what is absent from it, in particular the cloak of allegory, which, whatever its merits elsewhere, has no role to play in lyric poetry. With Villon nothing stands between the writer and the reader. Could this, after all, be the explanation of 'la vie mystérieuse et magique de la poésie' which Siciliano finds in Villon's verse and not in that of his contemporaries?

*

Despite its intricacies and contradictions, Villon's poetry, taken as a whole, has a pattern, owed not to any conscious planning, but to the fact that it reflects his own moods and feelings throughout their many changes. If he had a message to give to other poets, it would be: live your poetry, never get it out of books:

> Travail mes lubres sentemens,
> Esguisez comme une pelote,
> M'ouvrit plus que tous les Commens
> D'Averroÿs sur Aristote.   (T 93-6)

Lyric poetry worthy of the name is bound to leave us with some idea of the man. Villon's real flights of lyricism may be short and fitful, he may on occasions be trivial, obscene or merely boring; the remarkable fact is that throughout he shows an interest in the living world around him, not in order to demonstrate what life might be if all were to resist vice, or if all were to scorn virtue. He is concerned largely with people as they actually appear in his eyes, for his outlook is inevitably coloured by his own plight and prejudices. He sees and judges the social ladder from the lower rungs. He gives us a frankly subjective view of his fellows, but, over and above these preoccupations with the individual, there emerges from Villon's verse a compassion for Man, which no other lyric poet of medieval France had shown. This aspect of Villon's poetry, implicit rather than explicit, belonging more to its spirit than to any precise details of wording, syntax, etc., has already received the attention of at least one critic: 'S'il est vrai que la Renaissance ait consisté, entre autres découvertes, en celle de l'Homme, il nous semble que Villon a poussé une antenne dans cette direction. Au cours du Moyen Âge nous ne voyons pas d'autre poète (sauf peut-être Charles d'Orléans) chez qui, de façon implicite mais poignante, retentisse ainsi le: Que suis-je?'[1] Villon's self-seeking, however, is very different from that of a Montaigne; it is that of a poet, not of a scholar, far less painstaking in its study of the manifold facets of the personality, but in another way more profound in that it deals simply and directly with feelings which are bound to form the core of any human life; it is a synthesis rather than an analysis; very different in another way too, for Villon's temperament was fundamentally that of an extrovert, 'ung bon follastre', 'un joyeux drille', and any account of himself is soon expanded to include others. Despite the great differences between Villon and the scholars of the sixteenth century, a very suitable epigraph to his poetry would be provided by Montaigne's aphorism: 'Chaque homme porte en soi la forme entière de l'humaine condition.'

It is fitting that Villon's works, coming as they do at the end of the Middle Ages, should provide so many themes of medieval French poetry with their apotheosis. No other age

[1] Louis Cons, *État présent des études sur Villon* (Paris, 1936), p. 137

had been so afraid of originality, so timorous of innovation. In the realm of lyric verse, the long-established rules of the courtly school were faithfully followed by the majority. This is not to deny to the courtly school qualities of its own, but for all its grace and charm they are not primarily lyric qualities. The emotions portrayed tend so often to be stereotyped. The original poets of the Middle Ages are to be found on the fringe of society, amongst those who had little or nothing to lose by ignoring the dictates and conventions of the courts: Rutebeuf and Colin Muset in the thirteenth century, Jean de Meun, too, if his inspiration had been a lyrical one, and Villon in the fifteenth century. Others, it is true, came to write lyric verse, as did Villon, largely through force of circumstance, but they are usually wrapped up in their own private grief. Such a one was Christine de Pisan, whose verse was normally didactic and moralising, occasionally pleasantly light-hearted, but who had her moments of lyricism when reflecting on her sorry plight, left a widow at an early age:

> Seulete sui et seulete vueil estre,
> seulete m'a mon douz ami laissiee,
> seulete sui sanz compaignon ne maistre,
> seulete sui dolente et courroucee,
> seulete sui en langueur mesaisiee,
> seulete sui plus que nulle esgaree,
> seulete sui sans ami demouree.

Another was Jean Régnier, a man of affluence whose verse normally bore the courtly stamp, but who, imprisoned and unable to pay the huge ransom, came near to sounding a genuine note of lyricism, more petulant, however, than pathetic:

> Helas, j'ay usé en ma jeunesse
> A vivre si joyeusement,
> Et il fauldra qu'en ma vieillesse

Vive en peine et tourment,
Et que je perde esbatement,
Joye, soulas avec lyesse . . .

A third, Guillaume Alexis, was more at home in the writing
of long tirades attacking the 'vieilles maquerelles' who corrupt
young women and break up marriages, but he too had his
moments of self-accusation in old age, and attained a quaint
and superficial form of stoicism:

Je pensoye en ma jeunesse
Ou j'ay mal employé mon temps;
Et considerant que vieillesse
Me vient assaillir, je l'attens . . .

Eustache Deschamps, always rather on the prolix side, was
upset at the changes wrought by time on his person, and gives
us a detailed, self-mocking account:

Devenus suis maigres, pelez, frilleux,
Po voyant, sourt, sec, annuieux, chargent,
Tousseux, roingneux, graveleux et gouteux,
Courbes du corps, po mangent, trop buvent . . .

Henri Baude wrote on the anguish of a broken heart:

J'ay autresfois blasmé en ma jeunesse
Jeunes amans, par grant desrision,
Du mal d'amours qui a present me blesse
Dont a present j'ay grant compassion;
Et croy qu'il n'est douleur ne passion
Plus dolente ne qu'homme peust soufrir,
Quant deux amans d'une complexion
Sont anexez, et puis fault despartir.

One of the great themes of lyric poetry is present here, but
who would think so? These lines awaken no response in the
reader. Why? Partly perhaps because Baude is not writing

about himself. The words are uttered by a literary creation of his whom he never inspires with life as does Villon his Heaul-mière. When Villon writes, ostensibly for another man:

> Deux estions, et n'avions qu'ung cuer . . .   (*T* 985)

he is once more living his poetry, projecting himself. He is able to recreate himself in the image of others. Not so Baude.

William Dunbar, the 'old Scots makar', had his moments of despair too, not so much in old age like Deschamps, but 'when he was seik':

> I that in heill wes and gladnes,
> Am trublit now with gret seiknes,
> And feblit with infermite:
> Timor mortis conturbat me.
>
> Our plesance here is all vane glory,
> This fals world is but transitory,
> The flesche is brukle, the Fend is sle,
> Timor mortis conturbat me.

The poem quickly turns into a sort of rhymed *danse macabre* with moralisations on the world's vanity. The Goliardi, writing in their dog Latin, had also composed lyric verse of a retrospective nature:

> Dives eram et dilectus,
> Inter pares praeelectus;
> Modo curvat me senectus,
> Et aetate sum confectus . . .

Though the court poet Charles d'Orléans never stooped to such menial confessions, he did compose several *rondeaux*, generally allegorical, on his old age, always with that delightful old-fashioned grace and charm and distinguished manner so characteristic of him:

144

Salués moy toute la compaignie
Ou a present estez a chiere lye,
Et leur dites que voulentiés seroye
Avecques eulx, mais estre n'y pourroye,
Pour Vieillesse qui m'a en sa Ballie . . .

In Charles d'Orléans and others, one encounters qualities
different from those of Villon. Yet, no matter how widely
one casts the net, no matter how abundant one's catch may be,
the results are always the same. Alone of all medieval lyric
poets of France, Villon breaks through the carapace of personal emotions, spreading and universalising his feelings,
attaining in the end to a vision, fleeting and imperfect though
it may be, of Man.

*

There is, in Villon's poetry, an interplay between the
microcosm on the one hand, the tiny, insignificant individual
with whom he is so concerned, whether it be his arch-villain
Perrenet de la Barre, Thibault d'Aussigny Bishop of Orléans,
his late friend Colin Cayeux, his mother or his foster-father,
Jacques Cuer, Jehan Cotart, Ythier Marchant, Pierre Saint
Amant, Denis Hesselin . . .—what a multitude of individuals
there is in his work!—and on the other hand the macrocosm,
the vision which comes to him at rare moments of suffering
and self-questioning, of mankind united in its ultimate miseries,
as the little individuals crowd, all of them, through the grim
gate of death. Finally comes the Christian vision of man
helping man through prayer to God, forming a bond so
strong that it transcends even death itself.

In the last resort, there is about the poetry of Villon a
nobleness arising out of the sordid stuff of his life. His own
paltry circumstances lead him to a vision of an infinitely
greater, and more splendid, reality.

145

Conclusion

STYLISTIC analysis of Villon's poetry confirms its closeness to
life: words and expressions suggestive more of the spoken
language than of the written language, the poetry turned so
often into a conversation, the rhythms those of a speaker, with
constantly varying distribution of stress and emphasis despite
the rigid nature of the verse patterns, the lack of the pre-
conceived plan usually found in literary works, the numerous
digressions, the images strikingly visual, concerned with things
seen and observed, not abstract literary figures of speech.
Everything points to its closeness to the man, its faithful reflection of his temperament. Of no writer would it be truer to
say: 'Le style, c'est l'homme'.

Although, as stated in an earlier chapter, an analysis of this
nature must be above all an end in itself, it does serve to explain
why Villon's poetry is so much more alive than that of his
contemporaries and predecessors who have written on the
same themes, and also it has some bearing on those modern
attitudes towards Villon mentioned elsewhere. It makes it
increasingly difficult, for example, to sympathise with the view
that the *Testament* is really two works in one, the farce belonging, like the *Lais*, to his youth, the lyrical regrets to his old age,
for this rationalisation fails to take into account the stylistic
peculiarities of Villon's poetry, and seeks outside the verse
itself explanations for its apparent incoherence which can in
fact be found in the innermost nature of the poetry. It also
becomes increasingly difficult to accept the contention that in

his lyric verse he is merely striking an attitude in order to deceive the reader. One thing he is incapable of doing is to stand aloof from his verse. His own emotions are directly involved in all that he writes, be it a mood of farce and buffoonery or one of sorrow and regret. This is true even when he declares that he has wronged nobody, for he believes very firmly in his own innocence, however mistaken he may be; self-pity is a very cunning and deceptive force, but it does not necessarily spell hypocrisy. The only exception where he is deliberately deceitful, is in his remarks on love; his posings as a 'spurned and cast-off lover' are part of the clown's costume, although they are certainly not a complete fiction. In his passages of melancholy he really is expressing his own feelings and not just weaving subtly deceptive patterns of words across the page. In the same way, in his satirical verse the gibe is on the tip of his tongue as well as in his poetry, the sharp mockery is in the look of his eye as well as in what he has set down, the merriment is in the curl of his lips as well as in his written word.

One wonders what that critic meant who declared that Villon was unfortunate in that he wrote in an age of futility, characterised by the want of—amongst other things—good stories and romances from which to draw his material.[1] Villon writes only about himself and those around him and reveals not the slightest interest in fiction as such. His earliest work—*Le Roman du Pet au Deable*—has disappeared,[2] but it too had its roots in reality, the 'Pet au Deable' being a large stone, 'une diverse grosse pierre de merveilleuse façon' according to a contemporary of Villon, belonging to an hotel in Paris, which was 'captured' by students in one of their pranks in

---

[1] W. P. Ker, *Form and Style in Poetry*, ed. R. W. Chambers (London, 1928), p. 81

[2] Villon may never have got as far as writing this work, in fact. See above p. xxi, note 1.

the year 1451, precisely when Villon was studying at the Sorbonne. No matter what the mood—and his work embraces many very different ones—he draws his material all the time from the life within and about him.

The living force of Villon's poetry is revealed quite differently in its constant progression of thought. This can be seen in the sequence of three *ballades*—the *Ballade des Dames du Temps Jadis*, the *Ballade des Seigneurs du Temps Jadis* and the *Ballade en vieil Langage Françoys*—which deal with the same basic theme: 'Ubi sunt qui ante nos in mundo fuere?' The last two are usually looked upon as mere pale reflections of the first, for, it is said, Villon's aim was to exploit this theme to the utmost. Thus the *Ballade des Dames* is, according to Wyndham Lewis, 'one of the towering poems of the world', whereas the *Ballade des Seigneurs* is 'a piece of verse comparatively inferior',[1] and the third *ballade* of the series sinks even further, for it is 'bald, dry and of little value'.[2] Gaston Paris was even more severe, finding the *Ballade des Seigneurs* 'insignifiante' and the *Ballade en vieil Langage Françoys* 'tout à fait médiocre'.[3] More recently, Leo Spitzer has taken up the same basic attitude: 'Tout ce qui était suggestion rêveuse dans la première ballade est devenu ici plate déclaration à la manière prédicante du Moyen Âge. . . . Non vraiment, ici Villon doit avoir «dormité»'.[4]

Uninspiring though the *Ballade des Seigneurs* may indeed be from the aesthetic point of view, to consider it merely as an unsuccessful attempt to prolong the reverie of the *Ballade des Dames* is to ignore the spirit of the *Testament* at this juncture, a spirit characterised by a continuously developing line of thought on death in which each *ballade* plays its part.[5] The

[1] op. cit., p. 240   [2] op. cit., p. 242
[3] op. cit., p. 113   [4] op. cit., p. 18
[5] See J. Fox, 'A Note on Villon's *Ballade des Seigneurs du Temps Jadis*' in *Modern Language Review*, July 1960, pp. 414-17.

musings on the *Dames du Temps Jadis* reach a poignant climax
in the concluding lines of the third and last stanza:

> Ou sont ilz, ou, Vierge Souvraine?
> Mais ou sont les neiges d'antan?   (*T* 351-2)

The envoi which follows drives home the lesson that such
musings can only lead to this unanswerable refrain:

> Prince, n'enquerrez de sepmaine
> Ou elles sont, ne de cest an,
> Qu'a ce reffrain ne vous remaine:
> Mais ou sont les neiges d'antan?[1]   (*T* 353-6)

Question must be answered with question, for it is inevitable
that there should be no other reply. This *diminuendo* pattern
sets the tone for the next *ballade*, so closely linked to the first
that we are obviously discouraged by the poet from lifting
the one or the other out of the context:

> Qui plus, ou est le tiers Calixte,
> Dernier decedé de ce nom,
> Qui quatre ans tint le papaliste?
> Alphonce le roy d'Arragon,
> Le gracieux duc de Bourbon,
> Et Artus le duc de Bretaigne,
> Et Charles septiesme le bon?
> Mais ou est le preux Charlemaigne?   (*T* 357-64)

The brisk and businesslike ring of the opening conjunctional
phrase puts an end to the declining wistfulness of the last lines
of the *Ballade des Dames*. The pace is accelerated by the drier,
harsher sounds and by the introduction of a large number of
figures in the concluding lines of the stanza, including even
the refrain, without the longer descriptions, covering two or
three lines, which end every stanza of the *Ballade des Dames*
and which inevitably slow down the movement, giving it a

---

[1] For the reading *enquerrez*, see Burger, op. cit., p. 18

stateliness rising to a majestic climax in the refrain. Now this
pattern is reversed: three lines are devoted to the first figure,
and the remaining five each add a new victim to the *cortège*.
The gathering impetus drives home the lesson that it is futile
to reflect sadly and at length on the fate of the heroes and
heroines of the past: 'J'en passe et des meilleurs' Villon seems
to be saying.

The reference in the second stanza to:

> . . . le bon roy d'Espaigne
> Duquel je ne sçay pas le nom . . .   (*T* 370-1)

introduces a note of flippancy which grows out of the mood
of the first stanza: it hardly matters if Villon forgets the name,
for his argument is as clear without it as with it. Next it is not
surprising to find him turning aside altogether from his *danse
macabre*:

> D'en plus parler je me desiste;
> Le monde n'est qu'abusion.
> Il n'est qui contre mort resiste
> Ne qui treuve provision . . .   (*T* 373-6)

and the *cri du cœur* of the *Ballade des Dames*: 'Ou sont ilz, ou,
Vierge Souvraine?' finds here a clownish echo: '(Lancelot)
Ou est il? Ou est son tayon?'

The third and last *ballade* in the series—the *Ballade en vieil
Langage Françoys*—continues the same anti-climactic movement, increasing the pace progressively, abandoning the 'ou
est' theme for the blunt statement of fact: death swallows all,
and ending each stanza, appropriately enough, with a puff of
wind:

> Autant en emporte ly vens . . .   (*T* 392, 400, etc.)

Playfulness, besides being in the 'old' French, appears in
various expressions: 'De ceste vie cy bouffez' . . . 'Ont ilz bien

bouté soubz le nez?'...'S'ilz en sont courciez n'ataynez'...
So much has Villon come to realise the futility of revolt against
death that we now find him declaring, in an offhand manner
contrasting sharply with the passage on the horrors of dying
which leads up to the *Ballade des Dames*, that, as long as he has
had his fling:

Honneste mort ne me desplaist.   (*T* 420)

It has been suggested that the *Ballade des Seigneurs* is a
deliberate and frivolous parody of the *Ballade des Dames*,[1] but
the two are not diametrically opposed in this way, no matter
how great the difference in purely aesthetic values; the former
grows out of the latter in a smooth, unbroken development
whose downward trend from poetry to irony and cynicism is
motivated already in the envoi of the *Ballade des Dames*, and
as we have seen earlier, there is also a tinge of irony, though
of a different kind, in the second stanza of this *ballade*. The
Testament is very far from being a static work, and there is
little point in reproaching Villon with his failure to remain on
the rarefied heights of the *Ballade des Dames*.

Desonay has pointed to the importance of movement in
Villon's poetry: 'Le mouvement: avec Villon il faut toujours
en revenir là. A-t-on déjà remarqué que la ballade de la Grosse
Margot comporte une vingtaine de notations de geste, surpris
au vol? Et que retenons-nous du «bon feu maistre Jehan
Cotart», sinon sa démarche zigzaguante de bien ivre?'[2] This
is a very true observation which can be applied not only to
Villon's characters but also to the spirit of the poetry as a
whole. Villon does not simply set out to write on a particular
theme, whether in these three ballades or in others, in the
Ballade du Concours de Blois, for example, or in the *Débat du
Cuer et du Corps*. Each subject evolves in accordance with his

[1] L. Spitzer, op. cit., p. 18   [2] op. cit., p. 176

moods and temperament. The philosophy which emerges in the *Testament* is certainly not a profound one:

> Puis que papes, roys, filz de roys
> Et conceus en ventres de roynes,
> Sont ensevelis mors et frois,
> En autruy mains passent leurs regnes,
> Moy, povre mercerot de Renes,
> Mourray je pas? Oy, se Dieu plaist;
> Mais que j'aye fait mes estrenes,
> Honneste mort ne me desplaist.   (*T* XLII)

It is essentially the philosophy of a mind still young and immature, although the *Débat*, written shortly after the *Testament*, holds out some hope that more sober ideas would ultimately prevail. The constant movement of ideas, the changes of attitude, the restless self-seeking, contribute towards the life of the poetry.

★

If Villon's poetry still means something to the present-day reader, it is precisely because it does not move on a plane apart from life, in an artificial world of its own, in fashion one day, gone the next. It has aged, admittedly, but it has not passed out of fashion in the way that the fads of the *Rhétoriqueurs*, or the Romantics, or the Parnassians have done; and the two are very different things. It has been transformed by the passing years, but has not died away altogether. Both the feelings and the language in which they are couched are living forces, drawn directly from life. That is why Villon so often gives the impression of being: first of us all.

A Selective Bibliography

TEXT OF THE PRINCIPAL WORKS

François Villon, Œuvres, edited in the *Classiques français du Moyen Âge* series by A. Longnon, revised by L. Foulet (4th ed., Paris, 1932)

This edition gives the nearest approach which can be achieved at present to the original text of the *Lais,* the *Testament* and the *Ballades* excluding those in jargon. It should, however, be read in conjunction with A. Burger's *Lexique de la langue de Villon* (Geneva-Paris, 1957), where a number of textual emendations are proposed and a full glossary given, and also F. Lecoy's 'Notes sur le texte ou l'interprétation de quelques vers du *Testament* de Villon' in *Romania,* 80 (1959), pp. 493-514.

François Villon, Œuvres, edited by L. Thuasne, 3 vols. (Paris, 1923)

Despite a voluminous critical apparatus, this edition is not as authoritative as the preceding one (see F. Lecoy, op. cit., p. 493, note 1). Faulty readings have sometimes been allowed to stand (e.g. from the beginning of the *Testament* ll. 34, 38, 85, 138, 150, 180, etc.) and the notes, though often informative and helpful, tend to be discursive and beside the point, and on occasions are quite misleading (e.g. from the beginning of the *Testament* ll. 43 (see Burger, op. cit., p. 15), 106-7, 126, etc.).

TEXT OF THE BALLADES WRITTEN IN JARGON (OR JOBELIN)

The editions by A. Vitu, L. Schöne, P. d'Alheim and J. Marthold which appeared between 1884 and 1908, are unscholarly and cannot be relied upon. They give the impression of containing more information on the jargon than do more recent works, but in fact their translations and glossaries are based largely on conjecture. The only positive advance made in the study of jargon in this period was the publication by Marcel Schwob in 1892 of a *lexique* of the language of the Coquillards ('Le Jargon des Coquillars en 1455' in *Mémoires de la Société de Linguistique de Paris,* vol. VII (1892), pp. 168-83 and 296-320.

M   153

Les Ballades de Villon edited by P. Champion in *Les Sources de l'argot ancien* by L. Sainéan, vol. I (Paris, 1912), pp. 111-38

On the whole this is the best edition at present available, being to the *ballades en jargon* what the Longnon-Foulet edition is to the main body of Villon's poetry. The *Glossaire étymologique* at the end of vol. II (Paris, 1912) is helpful and gives meanings only when these have been quite definitely established. The text of the six *ballades en jargon* included in the 1489 edition by P. Levet is given, and also that of the five *ballades en jargon* of the Stockholm MS. which were published for the first time by A. Vitu in 1884. These latter cannot be attributed with certainty to Villon, as Champion points out (pp. 117-21), and even the one which carries Villon's name in acrostics may be the work of an imitator (see the remarks of M. Roques in *Romania*, 1955, p. 119).

L. Thuasne (op. cit.) reproduces in an appendix (vol. III, pp. 659-80) the six poems in jargon of the Levet edition and the *ballade* of the Stockholm MS. which carries Villon's name in acrostics, but no methodical study of the poems is attempted. Thuasne claims to have reproduced the originals faithfully, but is reproached by G. Esnault (see below, p. 155) with various faults, notably the omission of several words. Thuasne has added a brief glossary which owes much to Sainéan. In its turn, Thuasne's text is reproduced in an appendix by G. Atkinson (see below, p. 155), pp. 283-9, without translation.

François Villon, Les ballades en jargon du MS. de Stockholm, edited by R. F. Guillon (Groningen, 1920)

This is a good edition of the *ballades* of the Stockholm MS., but these are precisely the ones whose authorship is in doubt, as Guillon admits.

Le Jargon de Maître François Villon, edited by A. Ziwès (Paris, 1954; new ed., 1960)

This edition gives the text of the six *ballades* of the Levet edition, along with translations. This work bears much the same relationship to the poems in jargon that Thuasne's edition bears to the remainder of Villon's works. The notes are extremely copious but at times superfluous or misleading (e.g. the use of demonstrative *cel* with the limited force of the definite article is not specifically a trait of jargon, and is found long before the fifteenth century; *prins* was not necessarily a mere spelling for *pris*, since rhymes such as *prinse*: *prince* were common, etc.).

'Le Jargon de Villon', by G. Esnault, in *Romania*, 72 (1951), pp. 289-309

This corrects the reading of earlier editions for several passages and offers ingenious interpretations of a number of expressions from the *ballades en jargon* (notably nos. V, VII, VIII and IX of Champion's edition), but is by no means a comprehensive study of Villon's jargon, as the title might be thought to imply.

TRANSLATIONS OF THE PRINCIPAL WORKS (limited to a selection of those which have appeared over the past fifty years)

Like all poetry, that of Villon defies translation, since the meaning is conditioned by so many factors apart from the actual significance of the words (see above, pp. 76-7). The most sensible attempts at translation, in my view, are those which are limited to a literal prose rendering and which have no pretensions of conveying the rhythms and sounds of the verse, which can be appreciated only in the original. It should be noted that not a single one of the works listed below can be recommended unreservedly, either on account of misinterpretations or on account of paraphrase which throws little light on the original text.

The Testaments of François Villon, translated by J. H. Lepper (London, 1924; 2nd ed., 1947)

A verse translation, based on Thuasne's edition, unaccompanied by the French text. Some very debatable statements are made in the brief biographical study which serves as introduction (e.g., p. 3, 'In all his writings it would be hard to find a line accusing fortune or luck . . .' The explanatory notes are sometimes very misleading (the translator has not understood that Macée d'Orléans was a man, not a woman; also the Picart heretics were not inhabitants of Picardy, etc.).

The Works of François Villon. With text, translation, introduction and notes, edited by G. Atkinson (London, 1930)

The French text from Thuasne's edition is given with an English prose rendering opposite. A good introduction gives the main facts concerning Villon's life, a balanced view of his personality and an assessment of the meaning and value of his poetry. The translation is competent but by no means always reliable, (e.g. *T* 872 is not 'except my mother', but 'neither has my mother' (see below, article by E. Vidal). The significance of the whole of this important passage is altered as a result of the mistranslation. The translator has occasionally been misled by Thuasne (e.g. *T* 126).

The Poems of François Villon, translated by L. Wharton with an introduction by D. B. Wyndham Lewis (London, 1935; new ed., 1950)

A verse translation, based on Thuasne's edition, unaccompanied by the French text. Renderings of the *ballades en jargon*, based largely on conjecture, are included.

The Poems of François Villon, edited and turned into English prose by E. F. Chaney (Oxford, 1940)

A scholarly prose translation, along with the French text, which is mainly that of the Longnon-Foulet edition, although that of Thuasne has sometimes been preferred, not always justifiably. No notes are provided and the introduction is very brief.

The Poems of François Villon translated by H. B. McCaskie (London, 1946)

The Longnon-Foulet text is here reproduced, with an English verse translation opposite. This on the whole is the most satisfactory of the numerous verse translations, remaining as close to the original both in letter and in spirit as can reasonably be expected of a verse rendering, though there is inevitably some paraphrase. There is also an occasional mistranslation (*T* 87 is not 'until he dies', but 'until I die', see Burger, op. cit., p. 16) and the notes, though good on the whole, are not always sound (e.g. *L* 4 'avoir le frain aux dens' does not mean 'to settle down', but is the equivalent of the English expression 'to have the bit between one's teeth', cf. Burger's *Lexique*, under *frain*).

François Villon, Poems, including the Testament and other Poems, translated to the original verse forms by N. Cameron (London, 1952)

Based on Thuasne's edition, but only the English verse translation is given. The translator warns us that he writes only as a poet, not as a medievalist nor as a scholar of the French language.

The Complete Works of François Villon, with a translation by A. Bonner (London, 1960)

This American work gives the most up-to-date of the various translations, being based on the Longnon-Foulet text reproduced along with a good number of A. Burger's suggested emendations (see above, p. 153). The text of the poems in jargon appears to be largely eclectic, not being based entirely on any one of the standard editions of these poems. The idea of translating into free verse was very good, and the rendering as a whole is successful, but is marred by several blunders (*T* 179 'plus noir que meure' is not 'more black than ripe' (see above, p. 127); *T* 730-1 'Je crache, blanc comme coton, Jacoppins . . .' is not 'I spit gobs of phlegm as white as cotton', since *blanc* is singular and refers to Villon himself; *T* 473 'A qui que je feisse finesse' is not 'I occasionally deceived him', but 'whomsoever I deceived', i.e. 'even though I deceived others (I loved him truly).' The notes provide much interesting information, but are on occasions inadequate (e.g. in *T* 662 *est* is taken to be a copyist's error for *ait*, in accordance with Burger's suggestion, but no explanation or reference to Burger is given).

The disappointing feature of this translation is that it perpetuates the gap between the scholarly and the popular works on Villon by failing to take into account the numerous articles which have appeared over the past decade or so in various periodicals in which valuable light is thrown on the meaning of several passages of Villon's verse. It would be quite wrong to dismiss their contribution as so much academic detail of interest only to scholars. (See below, pp. 159-62.)

Adaptations such as those of the American poet, Robert Lowell, are not included here. They are often of considerable poetic value in themselves, but offer little help to students of Villon, except in so far as they capture the spirit, if not the letter, of the original.

CRITICAL WORKS

P. Champion, *François Villon, sa vie et son temps*, 2 vols. (Paris, 1913; 2nd ed., 1933)

This is the best work on the life and times of Villon. It is richly detailed, scholarly and authoritative. See also this same author's chapter on Villon ('Le pauvre Villon') in his *Histoire poétique du XVe siècle*, vol. II (Paris, 1923), pp. 57-131.

A SELECTIVE BIBLIOGRAPHY

I. Siciliano, *François Villon et les thèmes poétiques du Moyen Âge* (Paris, 1934)

The best study of literary themes in Villon's poetry, showing how great Villon's debt was to poets of the earlier Middle Ages. Invaluable, not only as a study of Villon's themes, but also as a survey of medieval French poetry as a whole. However, Siciliano's ideas on the composition of the *Testament* are debatable (see above, pp. 15-26) and his concluding chapters on the art of Villon as a poet, though written in a pleasantly lyrical style, are disappointing and contribute little to our understanding and appreciation of Villon's poetry.

F. Desonay, *Villon* (Paris, 1933; 2nd ed., 1947)

This modest little book dealing with the life of Villon and the nature of his poetry is very well worth reading, and is particularly interesting on Villon's art as a writer. It is, however, not a systematic study of Villon's style, but presents in rather desultory a fashion those features which have struck the author as being particularly significant.

L. Spitzer, 'Étude ahistorique d'un texte: *Ballade des Dames du Temps Jadis*' in *Modern Language Quarterly* 1 (1940), pp. 7-22

This brief but penetrating study of Villon's best-known poem should be read by all who are interested in Villon's poetry *as* poetry.

G. Paris, *Villon* (Paris, 1901) in *Les grands écrivains français* series

Although outdated in a number of respects (see above, pp. 14-15), this work retains its usefulness as a general survey of Villon's life and works.

L. Cons, *État présent des études sur Villon* (Paris, 1936)

A work of greater interest and importance than is suggested by the title. It is more than a bibliographical study, since the author expresses numbers of personal opinions, often perspicacious, though there are some questionable interpretations of certain passages. The author follows the history of Villon studies from the sixteenth century onwards, with particular attention paid to more recent times, up to 1936, the date of publication of the book. He devotes chapters to the work done on Villon in Germany, England, Spain and Italy, and is the first writer to cast doubts on certain aspects of Siciliano's work (pp. 119-33).

H. de Vere Stacpoole, *François Villon, his Life and Times* (London, 1916)
  As one might expect from the pen of the well-known novelist, this account of Villon's life is highly dramatised, though it is set against a solidly based historical background. The running commentaries on the *Lais* and the *Testament* which take up the second part of the work contain some shrewd comments, but there are several misinterpretations and bad misprints (e.g. 'Mourrez-je pas?' on p. 156). Superseded by the following work.

D. B. Wyndham Lewis, *François Villon, A Documented Survey* (London, 1928)
  The best-known of the English studies of Villon. A hearty, vivid, highly spiced account of Villon's life and poetry which makes entertaining reading.

C. Mackworth, *François Villon, A Study* (London, 1947)
  A biography of a popular kind, adding nothing new to what is known about Villon's life. Like Wyndham Lewis, the author gives in the concluding pages several passages of the *Testament* and some of the better known *ballades*, along with verse translations by various hands.

A SELECTION OF ARTICLES PUBLISHED IN THE DECADE 1949-59, throwing new light on various aspects of Villon's poetry

D. Legge, 'On Villon's "Testament" CXXIII' in *Modern Language Review* vol. 44 (1949), pp. 199-206.
  The reference is to the Scottish archers, who in Villon's time were frequently involved in brawls. Line 6 means that the Promoter called upon the names of God and Saint George, *maugréa* ('cursed') being ironical on Villon's part. The use of *gorge* in the more farcical works was apt to invoke the name of Saint George as a convenient rhyming word. The idea of his being named here as a Scottish saint is false. '. . . on some dark night long ago, a small band of men, amongst whom was probably a Scottish archer, who had a grudge against ecclesiastical authority, fell upon François de la Vacquerie and one of them went for his throat. In his terror he called for help upon God and the appropriate saint, Saint George. The event caused much glee in Villon's circle, and he bequeathed to him a plain Scottish neckpiece in commemoration' (p. 206).

H. Sten, 'Pour l'interprétation de Villon' in *Romania*, 71 (1950), pp. 509-12
   Deals with the identity of 'ma demoiselle au nez tortu', *T* 939; gives a new explanation for the difficult expression 'emprunter elles', *T* 448; the pronoun can be taken as the subject: '(the young prostitutes) who for their part are allowed credit everywhere (whereas the old ones are not)'; in *T* 157 the implication of *mesdit*, which some have thought to be a misreading of *mesfit*, may well be that far from *doing* anything wrong, Diomedes did not so much as *say* anything wrong.

J. Rychner, 'Pour le *Testament* de Villon (vers 553-5 et 685)' in *Romania*, 74 (1953), pp. 383-9
   The oft-debated lines 553-5 do not mean that Katherine is ugly and must seize any chance of getting a lover, but that beauty vanishes with age, and that the old prostitute, try as she may, can no longer attract anybody. The implication, as in the rest of the poem, is that the young women must gather hay while the sun shines.
   In *T* 685 *m'acouter* given by all the standard editions is a mistake for *sacouter*, 'to speak into somebody's ear'.

L. F. Benedetto, *Il dialogo di Villon col suo Cuore*, estratto dagli *Atti della Accademia delle Scienze di Torino*, vol. LXXXVII (1952-3)
   A detailed study of the *Débat du Cuer et du Corps* in which several textual emendations are proposed.

N. Edelman, 'A Scriptural Key to Villon's Testament' in *Modern Language Notes*, 72 (1957), pp. 345-51
   The psalm *Deus Laudem* (CVIII in the Catholic psalter, CIX in the Protestant version) to which Villon refers in connection with Thibault d'Aussigny (*T* 45-8) was very much in Villon's mind at the time of his writing the first part of the *Testament*, and is in effect a key to the understanding of these important lines.

R. Harden, 'Villon and his Monetary Bequests' in *Speculum*, 33 (1958), pp. 345-50
   The irony of Villon's monetary bequests is made all the greater by the fact that the coins he bequeathed to his legatees were practically unobtainable or had become illegal tender since the currency reform which followed the departure of the English from Paris.

A. Burger, 'L'Entroubli de Villon (*Lais*, H. XXXV-XL)' in *Romania*, 79 (1958), pp. 485-95

An ingenious explanation of the enigmatic stanzas concluding the *Lais*, which are, according to Burger, a veiled allusion to the robbery of the Collège de Navarre, the ringing of the Sorbonne bell (*L* 276-80) being the signal for Villon and his confederates to assemble, and the 'entroubli' following (*L* 281) being the actual time he was away on the robbery. The object, so far as Villon was concerned, was to enable him to present himself at the court of the Roi René at Angers: 'Il avait besoin d'argent pour son voyage' (p. 492). His story that he was planning another robbery at Angers was an invention on his part: '. . . . que Villon ait été affilié à une bande de malfaiteurs professionnels, c'est une idée romanesque qui ne résiste pas à une critique sérieuse' (p. 495).

J. Frappier, 'Pour le commentaire de Villon, *Testament*, vers 751-2' in *Romania*, 80 (1959), pp. 191-207

On the double meaning which the lines:

> Je les aime, tout d'ung tenant,
> Ainsi que fait Dieu le Lombart

had for Villon's own circle, that of the clerics of Paris. *Lombart* means 'money-lender', but can also be taken as a reference to Pierre le Lombart: 'I love all three of them together, just as Pierre le Lombart loves God (the Trinity).' (Syntax offers no difficulty, since both *Dieu* and *le Lombart* can be either subject or object.) The necessity of loving God as the Trinity was underlined in Pierre le Lombart's *Sententiae*, still well known in Villon's day, in clerical circles at least. Frappier sees in this interpretation a richer and more ironical meaning, the more so as the quip was directed against a *bishop* and his two legal representatives.

M. Dubois, 'Poitou et Poitevins (De Benoit à Villon)' in *Romania*, 80 (1959), pp. 243-53

On the significance of *T* 1054-69. Develops an observation made earlier by L. Foulet that Poitou had the meaning of 'soit un pays fictif, non existant, soit un pays où l'on dit non' (p. 248). Shows that 'Se je parle ung peu poictevin' can imply 'If I am talking nonsense, or saying something without meaning it'; hence the promise to pay Robin Turgis for his wine if he manages to find Villon's hiding-place is not seriously intended.

E. Vidal 'Deux legs de Villon' in *Romance Philology*, vol. XII (1958-9), pp. 251-57

'Ne ma mere' in *T* 872 does not mean 'except my mother', but 'neither has my mother'. 'Ma chiere rose' in *T* 910 is simply a sarcastic reference to Villon's mistress. Foulet and others were wrong in thinking that Rose was her name. The lines *T* 910-17 have in addition a thinly veiled obscene meaning.

F. Lecoy, 'Notes sur le texte ou l'interprétation de quelques vers du *Testament* de Villon' in *Romania*, 80 (1959), pp. 493-514. (See above, p. 153)

Proposes numerous textual emendations, the general effect of which, like those suggested by Burger in his *Lexique* (see above, p. 153) is to restore the reading of the best MS. (C).

Index

Abelard, 119
Agada, S., 81
Alexander, 20, 91
Alexis, Guillaume, 62, 99, 143
Angers, xv, 118, 161
Ars Amatoria (Ovid), 136
Art Poétique (Boileau), 2-3
Arts de Seconde Rhétorique, 47
Asne Royé, L', xvi
assonating rhyme, 73-6
Atkinson, G., 88, 154, 155-6
Atti della Accademia delle Scienze di Torino, 160

Ballade de Bonne Doctrine, 99, 102
Ballade du Concours de Blois, 75, 151
Ballade des Dames du Temps Jadis,
    xxii, 3, 35, 61, 62, 69, 77, 103,
    118-19, 148, 149, 150, 151
Ballade, Double, 62, 66, 68, 119
Ballade des Femmes de Paris, 61
Ballade de la Grosse Margot, 8, 11,
    32-3, 50, 54, 57-8, 67, 68, 74, 75,
    108, 117, 129, 151
Ballades en Jargon, Les (ed. P. Cham-
    pion), 101, 154
Ballades en Jargon du MS. de Stockholm
    (ed. R. F. Guillon), 154
Ballades en Jargon du MS. de Stockholm
    (K. Sneyders de Vogel), 102
Ballade des Langues Envieuses, 100
Ballade de Mercy, 86-7
Ballade et Oroison, 66-7, 68
Ballade des Pendus, xx, 28

Ballade pour prier Nostre Dame, 97,
    104, 120
Ballade des Proverbes, 101
Ballade des Seigneurs du Temps Jadis,
    148, 151
Ballade en vieil Langage Françoys, 148,
    150
Banville, T. de, 11-12
Baude, Henri, 143
Baudelaire, 17
Beethoven, 44
Belle Heaulmière, La, xxi, 68, see also
    Regrets de la Belle Heaulmière
Belloc, H., 114
Benedetto, L., 160
Bibliothèque de la Pléiade, La, 13
Blanche de Castille, 128
Boileau, xi, 2, 3, 4, 6, 7, 77
Bonnefon, D., 10
Bonner, A., 157
Boulogne, xvi
Bruneau, C., 41, 42, 92
Brunot, F., 41, 92
Burger, A., viii, xv, 52, 79, 108, 109,
    111, 114, 149, 153, 156, 157, 161
Buridan, Jean, 119

caesura in medieval verse, 48-55, 56,
    58
Cameron, N., 156
Caractères, Les (La Bruyère), 116
Carco, F., 13
Cary, H. F., 13
Cayeux, Colin, 145

163

Index of Line References

INDEX OF LINE REFERENCES

INDEX OF LINE REFERENCES

INDEX OF LINE REFERENCES

Printed in Great Britain by Robert Cunningham and Sons Ltd, Alva